Liberating Minds, Restoring Kenyan History

Anti-Imperialist Resistance by Progressive South Asian Kenyans

1884-1965

by

Nazmi Durrani

With Additional Material By **Naila Durran**i and **Benegal Pereira**

in Gujarati and English

Vita Books
Nairobi: 2017

T0319185

First published in Kenya by

Vita Books
2017

Vita Books
P.O. Box 62501-00200, Nairobi. Kenya
info.vitabkske@gmail.com; info@vitabooks.co.uk
http://vitabooks.co.uk

Acknowledgement for Nazmi Durrani's articles: Alakmalak (Nairobi)
Gujarati to English translation by Dr. Adam Tankarvi
Photos: Vipool Kalyani, Benegal Pereira Makhan Singh's Family/Amarjit
    Chandan
Cover Design by Heavyconcious Art Movement

Library of Congress Cataloging-in-Publication
Durrani, Nazmi.
Liberating Minds, Restoring Kenyan History: Anti-Imperialist Resistance by
Progressive South Asian Kenyans, 1884-1965 / by Nazmi Durrani.
202p. 14.8 x 21cm.

ISBN 978-9966-097-41-5 (print) and 978-9966-1890-3-5 (Ebook)
1. South Asians—Kenya—History. 2. Kenya—History. 3. Kenya—
    Politics and government. I. Title.
DT433.566.D87 2016

ISBN 978-9966-097-41-5 (print) and 978-9966-1890-3-5 (Ebook)

Layout, Design & Printed By www.vumacoolgraphics.com

Distributed Worldwide by:
African Books Collective
P.O. Box 721, Oxford, OX1 9EN
orders@africanbookscollective.com
www.africanbookscollective.com

મસ્તફ઼િક઼ મુક઼્તિ, કેન્યાના ઇતિહાસનું પુન:સ્થાપન

પ્રગતિશીલ કેન્યાવાસી દક્ષિણિ એશિયનોનો સામ્રાજ્યવાદ સામે પ્રતિકાર
૧૮૮૪ - ૧૯૬૫

ગુજરાતી - અંગ્રેજી આવૃત્તિ

લેખક

નઝ઼મી દૂરાણી

પૂરક લેખો: નાઈલા દૂરાણી અને બેનેગલ પરૈરા

ગુજરાતીમાંથી અંગ્રેજી રૂપાંતર: ડૉ. અદમ ટંકારવી

વીટા બુક્સ

2017
P.O Box 62501-00200
Nairobi, Kenya

http://vitabooks.co.uk

email: info.vitabkske@gmail.com; info@vitabooks.co.uk

વિશ્વવ્યાપી વિતરક :
આફ્રિકન બુક્સ કલેકટીવ
પોસ્ટબૉક્ષ 721
ઑક્ષ઼ફ઼ર્ડ OX1 9EN
ઑર્ડર@africanbookscollective.com

ISBN: 978-9966-097-41-5 (print) and 978-9966-1890-3-5 (Ebook)

Contents

Preface:

Shiraz Durrani: Arming People With Revolutionary History

An important aspect of the struggle against colonialism and imperialism in Kenya relates to the ideas, actions and tactics that informed and guided those who resisted exploitation and oppression of their country and people. Equally important is the recording, storing and dissemination of the information and history of these struggles. Colonialism and imperialism, with their control over media, education and public opinion are infamous in that they rewrite, misrepresent, distort, manipulate or remove from public domain records of revolutionary ideas, actions, organisations, leaders and events that they consider dangerous to their continued rule. A good example of this is the way British imperialism has sought to ignore, downplay or remove from history books people's resistance in Kenya. This process of the "theft of colonial history" is amply documented by Cobain (2016)[1]. This practice has been continued by the new ruling class after independence.

Thus it was not only the resistance by almost every nationality in Kenya (as briefly documented by Nazmi Durrani in this book) in the earlier period of colonialism that is hidden, but also the Mau Mau resistance in the last period of colonialism. They are not part of any school, college or university curricula. They are also ignored to a large extent by the mass media and generally pushed to the margins by Government policies and practices.

---

1. Cobain, Ian (2016): The History Thieves: Secrets, Lies and the Shaping of a Modern Nation. London: Portobello Books.

Similarly ignored is the contribution made by progressive South Asian Kenyans in the country's independence and liberation. Many of them paid with their lives for their opposition to colonialism and imperialism from the earliest period of British colonialism when Ghadar activists were put to death by the British authorities. Many others were incarcerated in Colonial detention camps for years.

South Asian Kenyans were active in their resistance in almost every field in Kenya: from publishing and printing of progressive books and newspapers to supplying arms and material to Mau Mau armed activists and supporting their families. Such support included supplying funds, information, services and arms to the fighters. In keeping with their infamous policy of divide and rule, colonialism and imperialism sought to isolate the South Asian communities from their African counterparts, and in particular, to isolate the progressive, organised South Asian working classes from their African class allies as well as from their own communities.

Many among the South Asian minority communities were used by colonialism, as well as the post-independence elites, as their agents to serve their political and economic interests. Within these minority communities, it was the progressive, working-class oriented individuals and organisations that had been singled out, harassed and punished the most by those in power. Some of those progressive people included individuals such as Makhan Singh, Pio Gama Pinto, Ambubhai Patel, Pranlal Sheth and Eddie Pereira, to mention just a few. Militant organisations and resistance movements such as the East African Trade Union Congress and Mau Mau were among those targeted by colonialism as well as those in power after independence. Their achievements, histories, sacrifices have been minimised, distorted, hidden or removed from official records of Kenyan history and their resistance has been stripped of its radical political and economic aims and achievements.

At the same time as there was resistance to capitalist economic exploitation and social oppression in general, there was a parallel resistance in the information and communication that documented and disseminated information regarding this struggle. South Asian journalists, printers, publishers and writers were active throughout the period of British colonialism in presenting Kenyan history from a progressive perspective.

The history of progressive South Asian activists may be sidelined or marginalised, but it cannot be denied its history. The material reproduced in this book is a testimony to this fact. The process of rewriting, preserving and disseminating such material has been helped significantly by developments in technology. Whereas in the past, printed works could be burnt, suppressed or allowed to go out of print, today it is possible not only to preserve oral and written records but also to disseminate them easily via the Internet. Records of people's resistance can now be kept and shared over a longer period of time and over wider geographical areas. However, technology also has its own shortcomings. There is a such a large amount of information shared on the World Wide Web that *relevant* information can easily get buried in this fast-flowing information surge, either deliberately or because of the sheer volume of information generated daily.

What this book attempts to do is to make available a selection of progressive information from an earlier, pre-Internet age of printed material and make it available to those who might have missed it or who were not around when the information was first published. Another important purpose of the book is to make such information available in a language other than the one of the original publications. Many of the articles in this book were originally published in Gujarati. Although spoken in India and around the world by over 65 million people, Gujarati is a minority language in Kenya. Thus the Gujarati articles reproduced in this book have been inaccessible to many Kenyan people whose national history they record. Similarly, they have not been available to a global readership keen to know about anti-imperialist struggles in Kenya.

There were a number of reasons as to why Nazmi Durrani had written the articles in Gujarati. First, it was an assertion of the rights of minority people to their own cultures and languages. Colonialism and imperialism have always sought to impose a single global culture promoting the use of English as a means of making easier the task of capitalist exploitation of global resources. Faced with this coercion, the act of writing in the language of the colonised people is an affirmation of the right of holding on to one's own language and culture. This pride in ownership and expression of their languages and cultures was equally important in an independent Kenya when the ruling class continued the colonial practice of divide and rule while using South Asian communities as scapegoats to mask their own elitist rule of self-interest.

Nazmi had other reasons too for writing in Gujarati. He wanted to reach out to people of his own minority ethnic community, the Kenyan Gujarati-speaking communities, to make them aware of their own progressive history. He was concerned to break the myth created by imperialism and its allies that South Asians were apolitical. Secondly, a year before his articles were published, his brother had been hounded out of the country by Government agents for writing a similar historical account, in English, of one of those heroes whose history Nazmi was recording, namely Pio Gama Pinto. In keeping with his political views, Nazmi decided that silencing history was not what Kenyans had fought for. He changed tactics and decided to record history in the form of his own choosing. He decided to write in a minority nationality language, Gujarati, and published the articles in a non-mainstream magazine, *Alakmalak,* thus escaping state censorship. Unfortunately, using Gujarati as a medium of expression prevented his writings from reaching a wider Kenyan population. In other instances, however, Nazmi wrote poems and other material in Kiswahili so as to reach the majority of the working classes in

Kenya. His collection of resistance poems, in Kiswahili and English, will be published in 2017 under the title *Tunakataa! (We Say No!)*. He had intended to have these articles published one day in English and Kiswahili. Sadly, there has been a long delay in publishing them, caused partly by Nazmi's untimely death in 1990 and partly by circumstances that prevented others from fulfilling this project.

The first part of the book consists of brief biographies of progressive South Asian activists by Nazmi Durrani. These were originally published in Gujarati in the magazine *Alakmalak* in Nairobi and in 2016 in *Opinion*. After a brief section "Remembering Heroes and their Achievements", the section "South Asian Kenyan Resistance" starts with an article by Naila Durrani, written in 1987. It was a paper presented at the Unity Conference of Umoja (the United Movement for Democracy in Kenya) when a number of Kenyan overseas political organisations came together in London to set up Umoja, a new umbrella organisation aligned to the underground Mwakenya-December Twelve Movement in Kenya. It is reproduced here to make it available more widely and also because it provides an overview to the historical articles by Nazmi, and in particular the class aspect of the anti-imperialist struggle. Nazmi Durrani's contribution in this section includes A Historical Review of South Asian Presence in Kenya and A History Reader which is written in simple language aimed at young people and provides a brief record of the resistance of Kenyan people of all nationalities against colonialism. It is included in this book to indicate that the struggle waged by the progressive South Asian Kenyans cannot be seen in isolation and needs to be seen in the overall context of people's resistance to foreign rule and plunder. Nazmi was working on yet another project, a photo-documentation of Mau Mau fighters and activists, before his untimely death.

This section concludes with an article by Benegal Pereira who provides background to yet another activist, Eddie Pereira, who was a prolific writer of letters to local press. Eddie Pereira's activism highlights another aspect of the struggles of South Asian activists: their battle was not only against colonialism and imperialism directly but also against the divisions they had created along class, race, cultural and religious levels within South Asian communities themselves. In addition to this complex situation, further divisions were created by the existence of different colonial powers, in this case the British and Portuguese colonialism each demanding loyalty to itself from the colonised people. Eddie Pereira was admirable in understanding, challenging and exposing these divisive imperialist tactics.

It is hoped that the publishing of this book will encourage others with similar records of the achievements of progressive South Asian Kenyans to document similar anti-imperialist struggles.

Acknowledgement

I would like to thank Vipool Kalyani for showing an interest in Nazmi's articles, reproducing them in *Opinion* and for his support in the production of this book. He introduced me to Dr. Adam Tankarvi who translated Nazmi's Gujarati articles into English. Without their support, this book could not have been published. The other authors, Naila Durrani and Benegal Pereira, also need to be thanked for making their contributions available for this book.

Of course, this book could not have been published without the contributions of Nazmi Durrani in researching and writing the articles reproduced here. Concerned with preserving them for posterity, Nazmi made certain of posting them regularly to London for safe-keeping.

Finally, a word of thanks to the many people in Kenya who helped to produce the book — the artists, designers, printers, proofreaders and many others whose input was crucial in producing this book. This is particularly important as it is the first Vita Books book to be published in Kenya.

Vita Books moves to Kenya

First and last pages of a publicity leaflet for Vita Books in 1986.

Vita Books was established in London, UK in 1986 to "publish progressive books on issues related to anti-imperialist struggles and to the establishment of just and democratic societies". The term *vita* in Vita Books needs some clarification as too often it is seen in the West as derived from the Latin for "life". As used here, however, *vita* is taken from Kiswahili, the national language of Kenya, in which it translates as "mapigano baina ya makundi, watu, wanyama, mataifa".[2]   In the Standard Swahili-English Dictionary,[3] *vita* is defined as "war, battle, fighting, contest, struggle".   We used it here to indicate a struggle for relevant information.

In addition, the term *vita* also relates to *vitabu* - Kiswahili for "books". And

2. Kamusi ya Kiswahili Sanifu (1981): Dar es Salaam: Oxford University Press. This give as an
    example of "vita": "vita via Majimaji - vita vilivyopiganwa mwaka 1905-1907 baina ya wenyeji wa
    Tanganyika na wakoloni wa Kijerumani".
3. A Standard Swahili-English Dictionary. (1955?): Oxford: Oxford University Press.

the dual aspects of its name — struggle and books — are captured in the Vita Books' logo designed in 1986 by Rahim from Design and Print (UK). Rahim also designed the 'Kimaathi' and other posters together with the earlier books which he printed from his workshop in Hounslow, UK. This is a belated acknowledgement of his creative work.

Over the years Vita Books has maintained this vision and continued its comparatively small publishing programme. It has now established its own website at http://vitabooks.co.uk

Over the years, Vita Books has worked with many progressive individuals and organisations. For a short period, it published books in partnership with the Mau Mau Research Centre, then based in New York. At the time of its establishment, it was intended that Vita Books should one day be based in Kenya which has provided it with its main inspiration.

The move has finally happened in 2016 and this is the first book to be published in Kenya. This move has been made possible by the enthusiasm and hard work of a number of people, including Kimani Waweru who will henceforth manage Vita Books from Nairobi. In addition, Vita Books are now distributed worldwide by African Books Collective (UK).

As Vita Books gets settled in Kenya, we hope to continue the *vita* in the information and knowledge fields.

Shiraz Durrani
October 20, 2016

આમુખ : વિપુલ કલ્યાણી 'શેષ ઝળહળ મશાલ'

અમારી આઝાદી માટે ભારતનો ફાળો નાનોસૂનો નથી, ભારત હંમેશાં રંગભેદ (એપાર્ટહૂડ) વિરુદ્ધ રહ્યું છે. આમ જનતાના અધિકારો માટેનું આંદોલન તમારા દેશે શરૂ કરેલું અને અમારી આઝાદી માટે તેનો ફાળો નોંધપાત્ર રહ્યો છે. અમે ભારતના ઋણી છીએ. તમે શરૂઆત કરેલી તેથી તો નેલ્સન મંડેલા કેદમુક્ત થઈ શક્યા છે. — ડેસમન્ડ ટુટુ

આર્ચબિશપ ટુટુની આ રજૂઆતમાં સત્ય ભર્યું છે. આછીપાતળી સંશોધનની પ્રવૃત્તિ હાથ ધરાતાં જ આવાં અરસપરસ આદાનપ્રદાનના અનેક દાખલાઓ ઇતિહાસે ભર્યા પડ્યા છે, તે સહજપણે વર્તાઈ આવે છે. જુઓને :

એલન ઓક્ટેવિયન હ્યુમ, નેલી સેનગુપ્તા, એની બેસન્ટ, ચાર્લ્સ ફ્રીઅર એન્દ્રુસ ('દીનબંધુ' એન્દ્રુસ), મેડલિન સ્લેડ (મીરાં બહેન), સેમ્યુઅલ એવન્સ સ્ટોક્સ - (સત્યાનંદ સ્ટોક્સ), બેન્જામિન ગાય હોર્નિમેન. હિન્દ્રવી જમાત માટે આ કંઈ પારકાં નામો નથી. આ જેવાં નામો - ભારત એક વિચારને પૂરાં વફાદાર - ભારતીય સ્વાતંત્ર્ય સંગ્રામમાં પૂરેવચ સામેલ હતાં જ હતાં.

તેમ અનેક વીર સ્ત્રીપુરુષો આફ્રિકાના મુલકોની આઝાદીની ચળવળમાં અગ્રેસર હતાં; અને આમાં દક્ષિણિ આફ્રિકિ અહમદ મહમ્મદ કાછલિયા, મો.ક. ગાંધી, ઇબ્રાહિમ અસ્વાત, રૂસ્તમજી, થામ્બી નાયડુ, યુસૂફ દાદુ, મણિલાલ ગાંધી, ઈસ્માઈલ મીર, યુસૂફ કાછલિયા, અમીના કાછલિયા, ફાતેમા મીર, અહમદ કથરાડા, ફૂરેની નોશરિ જીનવાલા, વગેરે વગેરે તેમ જ પૂર્વ આફ્રિકિ અલીભાઈ મુલ્લા જીવણજી, ઉછરંગરાય ઓઝા, મણિલાલ એ. દેસાઈ, સીતારામ આચાર્ય, ગિરિધારીલાલ વદ્દિયાર્થી, મખ્ખનસિહ, પિયો ગામા પીન્ટો, અંબુભાઈ પટેલ, હારુન અહમદ, પુરાણલાલ શેઠ, ડી. કે. શારદા, ચનન સિહ, કાન્તભાઈ પી. શાહ, અંબુભાઈ પટેલ, જશવંત સિહ ભારાજ, રણધીર ઠાકર, અમીર જમાલ, છોટુભાઈ સોમૈયા, રજત નયોગી, સુગરા વસિરામ, વગેરે વગેરેનાં યોગદાન આજે ય જોમ પૂરે છે.

માર્કસ ગારવીનું એક અવતરણ અબીહાલ, 'The Sultan's Spymaster' ચોપડીમાં, વાંચવા મળ્યું : 'પોતીકા ઇતિહાસની, નજીકી ઉગમની તેમ જ સ્વ-સંસ્કૃતિ વિષયક માહિતીવિગતની જાણકારી વિનાના માણસો જાણે કે મૂળ વિનાનાં વૃક્ષ જેવાં છે.'

આવાં કેટલાંક મૂળની તરતપાસ એટલે ડાયસ્પોરિક ઇતિહાસમાં એક ડોકિયું.

'કેન્યાનું સૌ પ્રથમ ગુજરાતી અને અંગ્રેજી માસિક' –ની ઘોષણા સાથે "અલક મલક" સામયિક કેન્યાના પાટનગર નાઇરોબીથી, 1985-86ના અરસામાં, આરંભાયેલું. સામયિકના માનદ્દ તંત્રી તરીકે પંકજ પટેલ હતા, જ્યારે માનદ્દ સહતંત્રી તરીકે રશ્મિ પટેલ હતા. તેનું સંચાલન અશ્વિન ડી. શાહ (વફ્રિકી શાહ) તેમ જ જે.કે. મુટુરી કરતા. તો મુદ્રણ સ્થળ 'આર્ટીસ્ટીક પ્રિન્ટર્સ' હતું તેમ જણાયું છે.

> આ સામયિકમાં નઝ્મી રામજી નામના એક અભ્યાસુ લેખકની કલમે કટાર આવતી. વિક્ટોરિયા સરોવર કાંઠે આવેલા કિસુમુ ખાતે 31 માર્ચ 1942ના રોજ જન્મેલા આપણા આ નઝ્મુદ્દીન દૂરાણીનું એક અકસ્માતમાં નાઇરોબીમાં 01 જુલાઈ 1990ના દિવસે કરુણ અવસાન થયેલું. નઝ્મુભાઈએ ગુજરાતી, કિસ્વાહિલી અને અંગ્રેજીમાં ય લખાણ કર્યાં છે. ખોજા પરિવારના આ નબીરાનું અવસાન થયા પછી, ગુજરાતી આલમે આ ઇતિહાસ ખોયો હોય, તેમ હાલ અનુભવાય છે. નઝ્મી રામજી 'ડિસેમ્બર ટ્વેલ્વ મૂવમેન્ટ' નામક ભૂગર્ભ પ્રવૃત્તિમાં ય સફ્રિયપણે સંકળાયેલા હતા અને કવિતા સર્જન ઉપરાંત પત્રકારત્વ ય કરતા રહેતા. વ્યવસાયે નઝ્મુદ્દીન શિક્ષક અને ગ્રંથપાલ હતા. વળી, કેટલાંક સામયિકોનું પણ એ સંચાલન કરતા. 'નઝ્મી રામજી' નામે લખતા, નઝ્મુદ્દીન દૂરાણી વિશેની આ વિગતો અને આ સમગ્ર લેખન સામગ્રી એમના નાના ભાઈ શિરાઝ દૂરાણીના સૌજન્યે પુરાપૂત થઈ છે.

'Mercantile Adventurers' નામક પુસ્તકની લેખિકા ડાના ઍપૂરવિ સીડનબર્ગને, એક મુલાકાતમાં હસ્સન નથૂએ કહેલું : 'One area we Asians have failed in is public relations. We don't know how to create a good image of ourselves.' [આપણે એશિયાઈઓએ એક ક્ષેત્રે નિષ્ફળતા મેળવી છે તે છે જાહેર સંપર્ક. આપણી સાચી છાપ કેમ ઊભી કરવી તે જાણે કે આપણને આવડતું જ નથી.]

એશિયાઈઓની આવી આવી જમાતમાંથી નઝ્મુદ્દીન દૂરાણી સહજપણે નોખા તરી આવે છે. એમણે સારી અને ખરી છાપ ઊભી કરવાનાં અનેક મજબૂત ઉગ માંડ્યાં હતાં. અને તેની શાખ આ લેખોમાંથી જડી આવે છે.

આપણી જમાતને નિરાંતવા તપાસતાં જણાઈ આવે છે કે વેપારવણજ અને વ્યવસાયીઓ વચ્ચે ક્યાંક ચડસાચડસી થતી રહી હોય તેમ લાગે જ લાગે. આવી સ્પર્ધા પૂર્વ આફ્રિકા ય મોજૂદ હતી. ઈતિહાસની નોંધોમાં ગરકાવ થતાંની જોડે તેના અનેક દાખલાઓ જડી આવે છે. નઝમી રામજીએ આ હરીફાઈને પાર કરતાં કરતાં પોતાનાં તારણો આપ્યાં છે. એમણે જાહેર જીવનમાં ખૂંપેલાઓની વાત ટૂંકમાં પણ મજબૂતપણે આલેખી છે. આમાંનાં ઘણાં નામો અન્યથા ભારેલા અગ્નિની રાખમાં ઢંકાઈ રહ્યાં પણ હોત ! આ જ નામો અને તેમનાં કામ તપાસીએ : મણિલાલ એ. દેસાઈ, સીતારામ આચાર્ય, ગરિધારીલાલ વદ્યિાર્થી, મખ્ખનસિંહ, પયિો ગામા પીન્ટો, અંબુભાઈ પટેલ, હારુન અહમદ, પૂરાણલાલ શેઠ, જશવંત સિંહ ભારાજ. આ સૌની આછીપાતળી વિગતનોંધ લેખકે એમના લેખોમાં મૂકી આપી છે.

આ લખાણમાં આવતું ગુજરાતી પણ તપાસવા જેવું છે. મુખ્ય પ્રવાહથી ક્યાં ય દૂર, કદાચ ત્રીજીચોથી પેઢીનું, અને પાછું મધુરું તળપદી ગુજરાતી વાંચવા પામીએ છીએ. અંગ્રેજી શબ્દોનો નહીવત્ ઉપયોગ, સાદા સમજાય તેવા શબ્દોનો વપરાશ એ નઝમૂભાઈને હસ્તગત છે. વળી એમનાં લખાણમાંથી પસાર થતાંની સાથે જગતના ઈતિહાસની પાયાગત સમજણ લેખકને કેટલી છે તેનો ય ક્યાસ આવવા માંડે છે. એમણે વિશ્વપ્રવાહોને ધ્યાનબહાર રહેવા દીધા જ નથી. અને તેની પછીતે એમણે આ ચરિત્રો આપ્યાં છે અને સમીક્ષા કરી છે.

આ ચરિત્રોમાં એમણે પુરગતશિીલ વચિારના કર્મશીલોને ય અગ્રસ્થાન આપ્યું છે. કેનિયાના માઉમાઉ આંદોલનમાં પૂરેવચ રહીને સફરિય ફાળો આપનાર અંબુભાઈ પટેલ અને એમના પરિવારની દેણગી ઊડીને આંખે વળગે તેવી છે. આ સઘળા સીતારાઓને કારણે એશયિાઈ જમાત માથું ઊંચું રાખી શકી છે, તેમાં કોઈ બેમત નથી.

આ લેખોનું સ્વાગત છે. નઝમૂદ્દીન દૂરાણીને એમના આ કર્મઠ કામને સારુ ઝાઝેરી સલામ.

પાનબીડું :

ઝાંઝ પખવાજ બાજ કરતાલ આજ,
સૂર ઘેઘૂર પૂર મત બાંધ પાજ!

બતિભૃખભાન, ઈબ્નબૂરજરાજ, વાહ -
જુગલસરકાર આજ મહેફ઼લિનવાજ!

તીર કાલદિ, શાખ કાદંબ તખ઼ૂત,
ફરફરે મોરપચિ્છ સરતાજ-તાજ!

અંગ રચ પૂરાસ, સંગ રચ રંગરાસ,

છોડ સગિર સાજ, તજ સરવ કાજ!

ભાન લવલેશ, શેષ ઝળહળ મશાલ,
શ્વાસ ઉચ્છ્વાસ ખેલ અય ખુશમિજાજ!

બતિ: પુતૂરી, ઈબ્ન: પુતૂર

– રાજેન્દ્ર શુક્લ
(ફેબરુઆરી, 1978)

e.mail : vipoolkalyani.opinion@btinternet.com
હેરો, 09-07-2016

Foreword:

Vipool Kalyani: The Flambeau Remains

"We owe our freedom in no small measure to India which is always against apartheid. Your country started the movement for rights and played a role in our liberation. We are thankful to the people of India. Nelson Mandela could come out of jail because of what your country had started". - Archbishop Desmond Tutu

These words of Archbishop Tutu are full of truth. Even a cursory glance at history reveals numerous examples of interaction, such as: Allan Octavian Hume, Nelly Sengupta, Annie Besant, Charles Freer Andrews (Deenbandhu Andrews), Madeline Slade (Meera Bahen), Sammuel Avans Stokes (Satyanand Stokes), Benjamin Guy Horniman – these names are no strangers to Indians. People like these, -fully committed to the concept of India – were at the centre of the Indian freedom movement. Similarly, many such brave people were in the forefront of the freedom struggle of African countries. Among these, Ahmad Mohammad Kachhaliya, M.K. Gandhi, Ibrahim Aswat, Rustamji Thamby Naidu, Yusuf Dadu, Manilal Gandhi, Ismail Mir, Yusuf Kachaliya, Amina Kachliya, Fatima Mir, Ahmad Kathrada, Freeny Noshir Ginwala etc. in South Africa and Alibhai Mulla Jivanji, Ucharangrai Oza, Manilal A. Desai, Sitaram Acharya, Girdharilal Vidyarthi, Makhan Singh, Pio Gama Pinto, Ambubhai Patel, Haroon Ahmad, Pranlal Sheth, D.K. Sharda, Chanan Singh, Kantibhai P. Shah, Jaswant Singh Bharaj, Randhir Thakar, Amir Jamal, Chotubhai Somaiya, Rajat Niyoji, Sugra Visram etc. in East Africa. Their contribution inspires people even today.

Recently, I came across Marcus Garvey's quote in *The Sultan's Spymaster*: "A people without the knowledge of their past history, origin and culture is like tree without roots'.[4] A search for these roots means a peep at our diaspora history.

In 1985-86, *Alakmalak* was launched in Kenya's capital Nairobi as "the first Gujarati – English bilingual magazine of Kenya". Pankaj Patel was honorary editor with Rashmi Patel as the associate editor. Ashwin D. Shah (Vikki Shah) and J.K. Muturi were the managers. It was printed at Artistic Printers.

Nazmi Ramji, a scholarly writer, contributed a regular column to this magazine. Born in Kisumu on 31 March 1942, Nazmudin Durrani passed away in a tragic accident in Nairobi on 1 July 1990. Apart from Gujarati, Nazmubhai has also wrote in Kiswahili and English. It seems, with the sad demise of this son of a Khoja family, the Gujarati community has lost this phase of their history. Nazmi Ramji was actively involved in the underground December Twelve Movement. Moreover, he was a poet and a journalist. By profession, Nazmudin was a teacher and a librarian.

He was associated with quite a few magazines and wrote under the pen-name of 'Nazmi Ramji'. These details about Nazmudin Durrani and the entire series of articles have been made available through the courtesy of his younger brother Shiraz Durrani.

In an interview with the author of *Mercantile Adventure*, Dana April Seidenberg, Hassan Nathoo said, "one area we Asians have failed in is public relations. We don't know how to create a good image of ourselves".

In this respect, Nazmudin Durrani stands apart in the Asian community. He took concrete steps to create a positive, true image of our people. This is evident in the present articles.

---

4. Aldrick, Judy (2015): The Sultan's Spymaster.?, USA: Old Africa Books. ISBN: 978-996675720

A close look at our community indicates that there was competition among businessmen and traders. Such competition existed in Eastern Africa as well. History is full of such examples. Nazmi Ramji has gone beyond such rivalry in presenting his observations. He has portrayed the people immersed in public life briefly but firmly. Some of these names would have remained unknown and hidden, buried under the ashes of time. Let us recall these people and their contributions: Manilal A. Desai, Sitaram Acharya, Girdharilal Vidyarthi, Makhan Singh, Pio Gama Pinto, Ambubhai Patel, Haroon Ahmad, Pranlal Sheth, Jaswant Singh Bharaj. The writer has presented sketches of all these people in his articles.

The Gujarati language used in these articles is also worth examining. We come across the language three or four generations removed from the mainstream Gujarati, and yet it is sweet and has a rural flavour. It is not littered with too many English words. Nazmubhai has the knack of using simple comprehensible words. Going through his writings, we can also fathom the depth of his insight into the world history. He never loses sight of international trends which he uses as the backdrop of these character sketches These sketches prominently portray progressive activists. The central role played by Ambubhai Patel and his family in the Mau Mau movement is striking. There is no doubt that the Indian community can hold its head high because of these shining stars.

I welcome this volume and salute Nazmudin Durrani for his spirited, vigorous endeavour.

Betel leaf:

Little consciousness, only the glittering flambeau, play the breathing, o, jovial!

- Rajendra Shukla

Nazmi Durrani:

Biographies of Progressive South Asian Kenyans

The Series by Nazmi Durrani was published in Gujarati in the Nairobi Magazine, *Alakmalak* in 1985-86. It was republished in 2016 in *Opinion Online Gujarati Thoughts Journal. Available at: http://*opinionmagazine.co.uk/subcategory/7/history [Accessed on 30-5-2016]

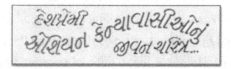

મણિલાલ એ. દેસાઈ (૧૮૭૮ - ૧૯૨૬)

મણિલાલ એ. દેસાઈનો જન્મ ૧૮૭૮માં સુરતમાં થયો હતો. ભારતમાં નિશાળ પતાવી તેઓએ વકીલાતનો અભ્યાસ શરૂ કર્યો અને ત્યાં નોકરી કરી. ૧૯૧૫માં તેઓ કેન્યા આવ્યા અને એક વકીલોની અંગ્રેજી પેઢીમાં કામ શરૂ કર્યું. જેમ દેશભરમાં અંગ્રેજ સામ્રાજ્ય સરકારે જાતિય ભેદભાવ સ્થાપિત કરેલ તેમ આ વકીલોની કચેરીમાં પણ આવા ભેદભાવનો અનુભવ દેસાઈને થયો. આવી વર્તણુકને તેઓ સહન ન કરી શક્યા અને કામમાંથી રાજીનામું આપી દીધું.

તેઓએ રીવર રોડ ઉપર એક નાનકડી દુકાન ખોલી. પરંતુ વેપાર કરતાં તેઓનું ધ્યાન વધારે કેન્યાની રાષ્ટ્રીય આંદોલન અને કેન્યાવાસી એશિયનોના હકોની માંગ માટે જે ઝુંબેશ ચાલી રહી હતી, તેમાં ખેંચાયું અને તેઓ ઇન્ડિયન એસોશિયશનના કામમાં લાગી ગયા. ૧૯૧૭માં તેઓ નાઇરોબી મ્યુનિસિપિલ કાઉન્સીલમાં કેન્યાવાસી એશિયનના પ્રતિનિધિતરીકે દાખલ થયા.

કેન્યા આવ્યા પહેલાં દેસાઈને ભારતમાં અંગ્રેજી સામ્રાજ્યશાહી વિરુદ્ધ જે જોરદાર આંદોલન ચાલુ હતું તેનો અનુભવ હતો. અહીં આવ્યા બાદ તેમણે જોયું કે ગોરાઓના શોષણ અને જુલમ જેવા ભારતમાં હતા તેવા જ આ દેશમાં પણ હતા. આથી બન્ને દેશોની લડતમાં પણ ઘણું ખરું સરખાપણું હતું.

વીસમી સદીની શરૂઆતથી કેન્યાવાસી એશિયનોની અંગ્રેજ શાસન પદ્ધતિવિરુદ્ધ લડત બે દરજ્જા ઉપર હતી. એક હતી મજૂરોની પોતાના હકોની લડત, દાખલા તરીકે ૧૯૦૦ની સાલમાં કેન્યાવાસી એશિયન અને આફ્રિકી મજૂરો તેમ જ નીચેના દરજ્જાના અંગ્રેજ કામદારો જેઓ રેલવેમાં કામ કરતા હતા તેઓએ ભેગા મળી એક હડતાલ કરેલ. ૧૯૪૧માં રેલવે સરકારના પબ્લિક વર્ક્સ ડિપાર્ટમેન્ટના કેન્યાવાસી એશિયન તેમ જ આફ્રિકી મજૂરોએ હડતાલ કરેલ. આ હડતાલના કારણે મજૂરોના નેતાઓ મેહરચંદ પુરી અને તીરથરામની ધરપકડ અંગ્રેજી સરકારે કરેલ અને તેઓને દેશનિકાલ કર્યા.

બીજી તરફ મજૂર નોકરિયાત અને વેપારી વર્ગોની સંયુક્ત લડત હતી કે જેમાં સામ્રાજ્યશાહીઓને બળજબરીથી આપણા મુલકમાંથી નિકાલ કરવાનો પ્રયત્ન હતો. ૧૯૧૪-૧૯૧૮ની લડાઈ દરમ્યાન આ લડતમાં ભાગ લેવાવાળા અનેક દેશપ્રેમીઓને ફાંસીની અથવા તો બંદૂકની ગોળીથી મારી નાખવાની સજા સામ્રાજ્યશાહી અદાલતોએ કરેલ. આવા દેશપ્રેમીઓમાં સીતારામ આચાર્ય અને બી. આર. શર્માનો સમાવેશ હતો. આચાર્ય ઉપર પરદેશી શાસન-સત્તા વિરોધી પત્રિકાઓની છૂપી રીતે વહેંચણી કરવાનો આક્ષેપ હતો.

આ સાથે કેન્યાવાસી એશયિન વેપારી વર્ગની લડત દેશમાં અનેક રંગ ભેદભાવ હટાવવાની અને રાજ્યનીતયિ હકો માટેની લડત હતી. આ લડત માટે તેઓએ ઇન્ડયિન એસોશયિશનની સ્થાપના કરેલ. આ વખત દરમ્યાન શાસન સત્તા એ ફળદ્રુપ જમીન ઉપર વલિાયતી એટલે કે ગોરા વસાહતોની જ માલકિ હોય એવો ઠરાવ પસાર કરેલ. આ સવિાય કામ, પગાર, શહેરમાં રહેવાના ઇલાકા, ભણતર વગેરેમાં રંગભેદ ભાવ લાવવામાં આવ્યા હતા જેથી વલિાયતી વસાહતોનો પક્ષપાત થાય અને આફ્રકિી દેશવતનીઓ અને કેન્યાવાસી એશયિનોના હતો સાચવવામાં જ ન આવે.

આવા ભેદભાવ સામે ઇન્ડયિન એસોશયિશનની લડત હતી. આમાં દેસાઇએ પૂરેપૂરો ભાગ લઈ આ લડતને ઘણી વધારે જોરદાર બનાવી. તેઓએ બી. એસ. વર્મા., શમસુદીન, હુસૈન સુલેમાન, વીરજ, સી. જે. અમીન અને મંગળ દાસ સાથે મળી ઇન્ડયિન એસોશયિશનને સારા પાયે સંગઠતિ કરી.

દેસાઇએ સર્વ પ્રથમ આફ્રકિાવાસી એશયિનોની એકતા માટે કેન્યા સવિાય યુગાન્ડા, ટાંગાનકિા અને ઝાંઝીબારના નેતાઓને ભેગા કરી ઇસ્ટ આફ્રકિન ઇન્ડયિન નેશનલ કોંગ્રેસનો પણ નવેસર પ્રચાર કર્યો. તેઓ કોંગ્રેસના પ્રમુખ ચુંટાયા. તેઓની નેતાગીરી હેઠળ ભારતની કોંગ્રેસ પાર્ટી સાથે પણ સંપર્ક સંધાયો.

આ વખતે સામ્રાજ્યશાહી અને વલિાયતી વસાહતોનો કેન્યાવાસી એશયિનો અને આફ્રકિનો વરુદ્ધિ પ્રચાર તેઓના કબ્જા હેઠળના ખબરપત્રોમાં પૂરજોર ચાલુ હતો. આ ખોટા પ્રચારનો સામનો કરવા માટે દેસાઇએ 'ઇસ્ટ આફ્રકિન કોનકિલ' નામનું સાપ્તાહકિ છાપું ચાલુ કર્યું. આમાં તેઓએ સામ્રાજ્યશાહીઓના અનુયાયો સામે પડકાર કર્યો. આ ખબરપત્રમાં તેઓએ આફ્રકિી જનતાની અંગ્રેજી શાસનસત્તા સામેની ફરયાિદોને પણ જાહેર કરવામાં મદદ કરી.

દેસાઇની કચેરી આફ્રકિી અને કેન્યાવાસી એશયિન નેતાઓને મળવાનું મથક બન્યું. તે વખતના આફ્રકિી નેતા હેરી થુકુ સાથે મળી તેઓએ આફ્રકિી અને કેન્યાવાસી એશયિનોના હકો માટે શાસનસત્તા સામે પડકાર કર્યો અને કેન્યાના રાષ્ટ્રીય આંદોલનમાં પૂરેપૂરો ભાગ લીધો. થુકુનું ખબરપત્ર 'ટંગાઝો' તેમ જ બીજી ઘણી પત્રકિાઓ છપાવવામાં દેસાઇએ તેઓને મદદ કરી.

૧૯૨૧માં અંગ્રેજી સામ્રાજ્યશાહી ગવર્નર એડવર્ડ નોર્થોએ વલિાયતી અને એશયિન વસાહતોના નેતાઓની એક પરષિદ બોલાવી, દેશના ભવષિ્યની ચર્ચા થાય અને ત્યાં આફ્રકિી નેતાઓ ન હોય તે દેસાઇને અનુકુળ ન લાગ્યું, એટલે તેઓએ પરષિદમાં આફ્રકિી અને આરબોના હકો માટે પણ જોરદાર માંગણી કરી.

૧૯૨૨માં એક અંગ્રેજ નેતા ચર્ચલિ વલિાયતી વસાહતોને ખાતરી આપી કે દક્ષણિ આફ્રિકાની જેમ કેન્યા પણ હંમેશ માટે ગોરા લોકોનો મુલક રહેશે. આ વખતે ગોરાઓની વસ્તી ૧૦,૦૦૦થી ઓછી હતી. કેન્યાવાસી એશયિનોની ૨૫,૦૦૦ અને કેન્યાવાસી આરબોની ૧૦,૦૦૦ અને આફ્રિકી દેશવતનીઓની વસ્તી ૨,૫૦૦,૦૦૦ની હતી. ચર્ચલિની આવી ગેરવ્યાજબી વાતને પડકાર કરતો દેસાઈએ અંગ્રેજ સરકારને એક તાર મોકલ્યો કે જેમાં તેઓએ કહ્યું કે કેન્યા આફ્રિકી મુલક છે અને અહીં ગોરાઓ અથવા તો એશયિનોનાં હતિ નહિ પરંતુ આફ્રિકી લોકોનાં હતિ સર્વશ્રેષ્ઠ હોવાં જોઈએ.

૧૯૨૩માં કેન્યામાં વલિાયતી વસાહતોનું જોર બહુ વધી ગયું હતું. તેઓએ કેન્યાને રૉડેશયિાની જેમ બળજબરીથી ગોરાઓનું સ્વતંત્ર રાજ્ય બનાવવાનું કાવતરું રચેલ. દેસાઈની નેતાગીરી હેઠળ કેન્યાવાસી એશયિનોના નેતાઓએ (જેવા કે એ.એમ. જીવનજી, રામશુદીન, બી. એમ. વર્મા. હુસૈન સુલેમાન વીરજીએ જોરદાર સામનો કર્યો. તેઓએ એક પ્રતનિધિમિંડળ લંડન મોકલેલ. ભારતથી પણ તેઓને સાથ આપતું એક પ્રતનિધિમિંડળ ગયું હતું અને તેઓએ ભેગા મળી અંગ્રેજી સામ્રાજ્યશાહી સરકારને ગોરાઓના કાવતરાને નષ્ફિળ બનાવવાની ફરજ પાડી.

આ વખતે હેરી થુકુની નેતાગીરી હેઠળ આફ્રિકી વરિોધ પણ અંગ્રેજ સામ્રાજ્યશાહી સામે ઘણો વધી ગયો હતો. થુકુ દેશભરમાં ફરી આફ્રિકી જનતાને અંગ્રેજી શોષણ વરિુદ્ધ ઉશ્કેરવાનું કામ કરતા હતા. આથી પરદેશી શાસનસત્તાએ ગભરાઈ જઈ માર્ચ ૧૯૨૨માં થુકુની ધરપકડ કરી. નાઈરોબીના મજૂરોએ પોતાના નેતાની ગરિફ્તારીની વરિુદ્ધ એક જબરજસ્ત મોરચો કાઢ્યો. નર્દિય સરકારની ફોજે આ બનિહથયિાર ટોળા ઉપર ગોળીબાર કર્યો, જેમાં ૧૫૦થી વધુ માણસો મારયા ગયા અને સેંકડોને ઈજા પહોંચી. ઈજા થયેલા લોકોમાં કેન્યાવાસી એશયિનનો પણ સમાવેશ હતો. આ બાદ સરકારે કોઈપણ મુકદ્દમા વગર થુકુને કસિમાયુમાં કેદ રાખ્યા.

દેસાઈએ ઈસ્ટ આફ્રિકન ક્રોનકિલમાં ગોરી સરકારના અત્યાચારને દેશ અને દુનયિા સમક્ષ રજૂ કર્યા. આ સવિાય તેઓએ થુકુ સાથે પત્રવ્યહવાર રાખ્યો અને થુકુની ઘરડી માને ઘણી મદદ કરેલ. થુકુની મા દેસાઈને પોતાના પુત્ર તરીકે ગણતાં.

ઈસ્ટ આફ્રિકન ક્રોનકિલની કચેરીમાં શાસનસત્તાના પોલીસે અનેકવાર ઘાડ પાડી. આખરે ૧૯૨૨માં સરકારે આ ખબરપત્રને બંધ કરવાની ફરજ પાડી. પરંતુ દેસાઈ, સીતારામ આચાર્ય અને એન. એસ. ઠાકુરે લડત 'ડેમોક્રેટ' નામના છાપા દ્વારા ચાલુ રાખી. તેઓએ 'મ્વીગ્વીથાન્યા' [Muĩgwithania (Reconciler)] નામના એક આફ્રિકી ખબરપત્રને છાપવામાં મદદ કરી. આના તંત્રી જોમો કેન્યાટા હતા.

૧૯૨૪માં બીજા દેશપ્રેમીઓ સાથે મળી દેસાઈએ પરદેશી સરકારને કર ન ભરવાની ઝુંબેશ ઉપાડી અને તે માટે સામ્રાજ્યોની જેલની યાત્રા પણ કરવી પડી.

૧૯૨૫માં કેન્યાવાસી એશિયનોએ દેસાઈને અંગ્રેજી લેજ્સ્લેટીવ કાઉન્સલિમાં પોતાના પ્રતનિધિ તરીકે ચૂંટ્યા. અહીં તેઓએ બીજા પ્રતનિધિઓ જેવા કે એ. એમ. જીવનજી અને બી. એમ. વર્મા સાથે મળી સામ્રાજ્ય સરકારની જાતિય ભેદભાવની નીત વિરુદ્ધ અનેક ભાષણો કર્યા. આ કાઉન્સલિમાં આફ્રિકી પ્રતનિધિઓ ન હોવાને કારણે તેઓની ફરિયાદોને રજૂ કરવાનું અને તેઓના હકોની માંગ કરવાનું કામ પણ દેસાઈએ પોતા ઉપર લીધું. ગોરી સરકારે કેન્યાવાસી એશિયનોની કોઈ પણ માંગને દરકાર ન આપી એટલે દેસાઈ, જીવનજી, વર્મા તેમ જ જે. બી. પંડ્યાએ લેજ્સ્લેટીવ કાઉન્સલિનો બહિષ્કાર કરેલ.

૧૯૨૬માં દેસાઈ, સીતારામ આચાર્ય સાથે 'ડેમોક્રેટ' માટે પૂર્વ આફ્રિકાવાસી એશિયનો પાસે પૈસા ભેગા કરવા સફરે નીકળ્યા. પરંતુ આ સફર દરમ્યાન તેઓ બીમાર પડ્યા અને ૪૮ વર્ષની ઉમરે, જુલાઈ ૧૯૨૬માં, બુકોબા, ટાંગાનિકા ખાતે અવસાન પામ્યા.

આ દેશપ્રેમીની યાદ કાયમ રાખવા માટે નાઈરોબીમાં એક સ્મારક 'દેસાઈ મેમોરિયલ બલ્ડિઁગ' બંધાવવામાં આવેલ કે જે અત્યારના ટોમ મ્બોયા સ્ટ્રીટ ઉપર આવેલ છે. આ ઈમારતમાં એક જાહેર જનતાની સભા ભરાય તેના માટે એક મોટો ઓરડો અને એક પુસ્તકાલય બનાવવામાં આવેલ. આનો કોઈ પણ જાતિય ભેદભાવ વગર સર્વ કોમના માણસો ઉપયોગ કરી શકે તેવી યોજના કરવામાં આવેલ. ન્ગારાના ઈલાકામાં એક રસ્તાનું નામ દેસાઈ રોડ પણ આ દેશપ્રેમીની યાદમાં રાખવામાં આવેલ.

વોઈસ ઓફ કેન્યાના કસ્વિાહીલીમાં પ્રસારિત થતા નેશનલ સર્વસિમાં ૧૨ એપ્રિલ ૧૯૮૧ના એક કાર્યક્રમમાં દેસાઈને અંજલિ આપતા કહેવામાં આવેલ કે :

"દેસાઈ એક એવા એશિયન હતા કે જેઓ પાસે કેન્યાના ઈતહાસને લાંબી દૃષ્ટિથી જોવાની શક્તિ હતી. તેઓ એક હિમતવાન નેતા હતા. તેઓને પોતાના અંગત સ્વાર્થ અને સુખની પરવા જરા પણ નહતી. તેઓની લગન અને લડત બસ એક હતી : સર્વ માટે ઈન્સાફ અને સરખાપણું."

સૌજન્ય : "અલક મલક", જાન્યુઆરી ૧૯૮૬; પૃ. ૨૨, ૨૩ અને ૨૭.

Manilal A. Desai, 1878-1926[5]

anilal A. Desai was born in 1878 in Surat District of Gujarat in India. After finishing school he studied law. He worked for a few years in the legal field in India and in 1915 migrated to Kenya where he was employed by a firm of British lawyers in Nairobi. Like in the rest of the country, there was racial discrimination in law offices too. Once when his European employer found him smoking at work, Desai was told that he was not to smoke in the office, that only Europeans could smoke there. Unable to put up with such blatant racism, he resigned there and then.

He then opened a small shop on River Road. However, he did not have much interest in running the business and he handed it over to his nephew after a short while. His real interest was in the anti-colonial politics of the country.

Background to class formation and class struggle [6]

Desai plunges into anti-colonial struggle

Desai's plunge into the anti-colonial struggle was via the Indian Association of which he became the Secretary. A.M. Jeevanjee, the pioneer trader, shipowner and building contractor, was its president at the time. Along with such other leaders such as B.S. Varma, Shamsudeen, Hussein Suleman Virji, S. J. Amin and Mangal Dass, he greatly strengthened the Association organisationally. In addition, he worked towards greater cooperation of all East African Asians. This led to the re-emergence of the East African Indian National Congress linking the Asians of Kenya, Tanganyika, Uganda and Zanzibar, the four

---

5. Nazmi Durrani wrote two versions of the article on M. A. Desai. This is the longer version.
6. This section has been moved to the section "Kenya People's Resistance in Context" in this book.

British colonial territories in the area. He became the President of the Congress.

The Asian Kenyans political struggle took a more militant path with Desai's entry. It now also stated looking at the colonial situation as a whole, and not merely from the perspective of the Asian Kenyan middle class.

Having had a first-hand experience of the anti-British colonial struggle in

India, he saw that the colonial exploitation and oppression in the land of his birth and in his adopted home were similar, even though the concrete forms these took in each country were different. This perspective had two results. On the one hand, he realised that the struggles in India and Kenya could learn from each other and also be strengthened if some sort of unity or coordination could be achieved since the two countries faced a common enemy, the British colonialism. For this purpose, he sought contact with the Indian National Congress.

Manilal Ambalal Desai

On the other hand, he took an active interest in the African anti-colonial struggle in which he saw similarities with the fight for independence that was going on in India. In the Kenya context, he realised that Asian Kenyans could not carry on their struggle in isolation from the African fight for their rights. In fact, he recognised from the outset that the African struggle was of primary importance.

Once having correctly analysed the colonial situation, Desai forged the instruments with which the struggle could be carried out. He saw publicity and propaganda as some of the main weapons with which the oppressed people could be informed and politicised for further action. The British colonial administration and European settlers used newspapers to propagate their interests. To combat this propaganda, Manilal Desai founded a Gujarati-English weekly, *East African Chronicle*. Through this paper he publicised African and Asian Kenyans grievances arising from the colonial racist discriminatory and segregatory practices. The paper also demanded political rights for the Kenyan Africans, Asians and Arabs.

Desai was instrumental in drawing the Asian Kenyans struggle closer to the African struggle. His *East African Chronicle* offices became the centre for the meeting of the leaders of the two communities. He worked closely with the Africa nationalist leader, Harry Thuku, who headed the East African Association. The two leaders, both bachelors, met during their spare time at Desai's place, which consisted of a single room on River Road which was provided to him by A. M. Jeevanjee. The *East African Chronicle* publicised the work of the East African Association, its protest meetings and also the African grievances and demands put forward by the Association. Among the issues it protested against were the appropriation of the African owned land by the colonial administration for the settlement of European immigrants; the compulsory registration of Africans and the carrying of the registration and employment papers in a metal container (the 'kipande') around the neck at all times; raising taxes without any government facilities being offered in return; forced labour on European owned farms.

Desai also published Thuku's Kiswahili paper *Tangazo,* and the leaflets and posters which publicised the public meetings organised by the East African Association. In addition, he helped Thuku draft a protest memorandum outlining the African demands. In July 1921 this memorandum was sent to the colonial government in England and to many overseas sympathisers of the Kenyan people.

In 1921 when the British colonial governor, Edward Northey, called a meeting of European and Asian leaders to discuss the country's future, Desai protested at the non-representation of Africans and Arabs at the meeting and made a forceful speech making demands on their behalf as well.

By 1922 the African protest against colonial injustices had reached a high point. Thuku and other East African Association officials were touring the country holding well-attended public meetings and demanding drastic changes in colonial policies. The colonial government was getting into a state of panic and on 14 March 1922 arrested Thuku and 50 other members of the Association. In protest against the arrests, the Nairobi workers called a general strike which paralysed the town. On 16 March, they organised a mammoth procession through the streets of the town. They gathered outside the police lines where Thuku was being held, at the site today occupied by the University of Nairobi. They called for his immediate and unconditional release. The colonial police opened fire on the unarmed protesters. Gun-wielding Europeans at the nearby Norfolk Hotel joined in the shooting. Some 150 people were killed and many more were injured. Among the first to be shot and killed was a woman leader of the demonstration, Muthoni Nyanjiru. The extent of the support for the protest among workers of different nationalities can be seen from the fact that among the injured were some Asians, as the *East African Standard* of 17 March 1922 reported. Following the massacre, hundreds of workers were arrested. The East African Association leaders, Harry Thuku, Waiganjo wa Ndotono and George Mugekenyi were deported without trial to Kismayu, Lamu and Kwale districts respectively. Among the many who were imprisoned was another leader of the Association, Abdullah Tairara.

In his *East Africa Chronicle*, Desai gave a detailed account of the whole episode, strongly condemning the colonial administration's ruthless handling of the incident. In conjunction with B. S Varma, Shamsudeen and Mangal Dass, he fought against the deportation orders and sought the release of the African leaders. While Thuku was in Kismayu, Desai corresponded with him to keep him informed about the developments in the country. The papers were forwarded through Thuku's Asian shop owner contact in Kismayu. He also kept in touch with Thuku's mother and helped her financially during her son's enforced absence.

For a long time, the colonial authorities had been looking for an excuse to close the *East African Chronicle*. On a number of occasions, it had raided the paper's offices looking for some incriminating evidence and to harass Desai and the other staff. Finally, in mid-1922 the paper was forced to close down. However, along with Sitaram Acharya and N. S Thakur, Desai carried on the fight in the pages of the *Democrat*. This paper at one time printed the Kikuyu Central Association's publication *Muigwithania* which was edited by Johnstone Kamau (later Jomo Kenyatta).

In the constitutional sphere, the European settlers during this period were pressing for self-government for Kenya under white rule. They demanded a constitution similar to that which the European settlers in the then Southern Rhodesia (now Zimbabwe) had been granted by the British colonial government. The British government in London, as well as the colonial administration in Nairobi, had always sympathised with the settlers' demand. In 1919 Governor Northey had proclaimed that "the principle had been accepted at home (i.e. in England) that this country was primarily for European development" and that "European interests must be paramount throughout the protectorate" (i.e. Kenya). In 1922 Winston Churchill, the Colonial Secretary, confirmed this undertaking given to the European settlers and went on to assure them that they could look forward to "in full fruition of time to compete responsible self-government" of "all civilised men". The measurement of the so called civilisation would be by "well-marked European standards".

The population of Kenya at this time was made up as follows:

Africans	2,500,000
Asians	25,000
Arabs	10,000
Europeans	10,000

Thus the destiny of over two and a half million people in the "self-governing" country would be in the hands of 10,000 white settlers. By 1923, it appeared that the fate of the country had already been decided upon. Desai, in a telegram sent to the British Colonial Office in February 1923, strongly challenged this policy. He said that Kenya being an African country, the interests of the Africans should be protected and that there should be "no predomination (of) European or Indian settlers".

In March 1923 the British government called a meeting in London to discuss the future of the country. The Asian Kenyans delegation, comprising among others of A. M. Jeevanjee, Shamsudeen, B. S. Varma and H. S. Virji was led by Desai. The British colonial government in India sent a delegation to the conference made up of non-official Indian members of the Indian Legislative. These two delegations opposed the European settler demands. African leaders were once again excluded. The leaders of the East African Association, in a memorandum sent with Desai, protested at their non-inclusion at the conference. During the conference itself, Joseph Kang'ethe sent a cable to London on behalf of the Association declaring that Africans "should not be handed over to a self-governing Kenya in which settlers predominate". All this opposition forced the British colonial government to back down.

In July 1923, in language reminiscent of Desai's February telegram, the Colonial Secretary, the Duke of Devonshire, declared that in Kenya "the interests of the African native must be paramount". However, having made this high-sounding pronouncement which came to be known as the Devonshire Declaration, the colonial government carried on with its earlier policies of total exclusion of African leadership from the political processes of the country and of racial discrimination favouring the European settlers.

In 1924, seeing that the money collected by the colonial administration was used to run the system that not only did not benefit the people generally, but was, in fact, used to oppress the very people who were paying these taxes, Desai organised a tax boycott. As a result he was jailed.

The following year Desai was selected to represent the Asian Kenyans in the Legislative Council, much to the displeasure of the colonial administration and settlers. He used this forum to tirelessly draw attention to injustices and discriminatory practices of the colonial authority and to challenge the racism of the European settlers. As the African population lacked a voice in the council, Desai worked closely with the leaders of the newly formed Kikuyu Central Association such as Joseph Kang'ethe, James Beauttah and Jesse Kariuki and presented their grievances and demands. Faced with the colonial administration's total refusal to pay heed to the Asian Kenyans representatives' demands, Desai, Jeevanjee, Varma and J. B. Pandya staged a boycott of the council.

Acharya and Desai faced enormous financial problems in publishing *The Democrat*. Lacking advertising revenue to run it on a commercial basis, the paper depended to a great extent on donations from those who supported its stand. In 1926 the two of them set out on an East African tour to raise money for the paper. Desai fell ill during the trip and in July 1926 died in Bukoba, Tanganyika at the age of 48.

The East African Indian Congress raised funds to build a monument, the Desai Memorial Hall, which stands on the Tom Mboya Street (formerly Victoria Street) in Nairobi in order to perpetuate the memory of this Asian Kenyans patriot. The building housed a library which, following the principle held dear by Desai, was open to people of all races. It was the first library, and for a long time the only one, in Nairobi to have such an open door policy. During the 1930s, 1940s and 1950s the meeting hall in the building was the venue for countless meetings of Nairobi workers. In addition, a street in Nairobi has been named after him, the Desai Road which links Murang'a Road with the Ngara/Park Roads junction.

A Voice of Kenya's National Service programme broadcast on 12 April 1981 had this to say about Desai:

He had the strength and foresight to take a long-term view of the history of Kenya. He was a courageous leader who did not care for his personal interests and comfort in the service of the cause for justice and equality.

મખન સિંહ (૧૯૧૩ - ૧૯૭૩)

મખન સહિનો જન્મ પંજાબના ઘરજખ નામનાં ગામડામાં ૨૭ ડિસેમ્બર ૧૯૧૩માં થયો હતો. તેઓના પિતા સુધસહિ સુથાર હતા. ૧૯૨૦માં સુધસહિ કેન્યા આવ્યા અને રેલવેની નોકરી કરી. ૧૯૨૭માં મખન સહિ અને તેઓનાં માતા ઈશર કૌર કેન્યા આવ્યાં.

સુધ સહિ રેલવેના મજૂર સંઘમાં મજૂરોના હક માટે જોરદાર લડત ઉપાડેલ. આ કારણસર તેઓને કામમાંથી રજા આપી દેવામાં આવી. પછી તેઓએ પંજાબ પ્રિન્ટીંગ પ્રેસ ખોલ્યું.

મખન સહિ નાઈરોબીની ગવર્નમેન્ટ ઇન્ડિયન હાઈસ્કૂલ(હમણાંની જમહુરી હાઈસ્કૂલ)માં ભણ્યા અને ૧૯૩૧માં લંડન મેટ્રીક્યુલેશનની પરીક્ષામાં સફળ થયા. તેઓને આગળ ભણતરનો બહુ શોખ હતો, પરંતુ પિતાની આર્થિક સ્થિતિ સારી ન હોવાથી એ વધારે ભણી ન શક્યા. તેઓ પંજાબ પ્રિન્ટીંગ પ્રેસમાં કામે લાગી ગયા. ૧૯૩૪માં તેઓ ભારત ગયા અને સતવંત કૌર સાથે લગ્ન કરી ફરી કેન્યા આવી ગયા.

મખન સહિને નાની ઉમરથી જ દુનિયવી રાજનીતિ અને મજૂર-કિસાન આંદોલનમાં બહુ રસ હતો. તેઓ આવા વિષયો તેમ જ કેન્યા અને ભારતની સામ્રાજ્યશાહી સામેની આઝાદીની લડત ઉપર પણ પંજાબીમાં કવિતાઓ લખી જાહેર સભાઓમાં જનતાને સંભળાવતા.

માર્ચ ૧૯૩૫માં મખન સહિ કેન્યા ભારતીય મજૂર સંઘ(કેન્યા ઇન્ડિયન ટ્રેડ યુનિયન)ના મંત્રી તરીકે ચૂંટાયા. તેઓ અને તેઓના બીજા સાથી નેતાઓએ જોયું કે મજૂરોને પોતાના હિતની રક્ષા માટે એકતાની બહુ જરૂર છે. ત્યારે સામ્રાજ્ય સરકારનો પ્રયત્ન હતો કે ભારતીય અને આફ્રિકી મજૂરો વચ્ચે ખટપટ રહ્યા કરે. જાતિય ભેદભાવ દૂર કરવા ભારતીય મજૂર સંઘે તેનું નામ બદલાવી કેન્યા મજૂર સંઘ (લેબર ટ્રેડ યુનિયન ઑફ કેન્યા) રાખ્યું અને તેનું સભાસદપણું સર્વે જાતિના મજૂરો માટે ખુલ્લું કર્યું. મખનસહિ આ નવા સંઘના પણ મંત્રી ચૂંટાયા.

મખન સહિની આગેવાની હેઠળ આ મજૂર સંઘને ઘણી સફળતા પ્રાપ્ત થઈ. ૧૯૩૫ની રેલવે સામેની ઝૂંબેશમાં તેઓ ફતેહમંદ થતાં રેલવેના કારીગરો કે જેઓ ઘણાં વર્ષોથી અનિયમિત મજૂરો તરીકે રાખેલ તેઓને કાયમી રીતે રાખવા રેલવેને કબૂલ કરવું પડ્યું.

એપ્રિલ-મે ૧૯૩૭માં મજૂર સંઘે નાઈરોબીના કારખાનાઓના કામદારોના પગારમાં વધારાની માંગ માટે એક હડતાલ બોલાવી. તેમાં પણ સફળતા મળતા મજૂરોના પગારમાં કારખાનાઓના માલિકોને ૧૫-૨૫%નો વધારો કરવાની ફરજ પાડી.

આ મજૂર સંઘ પૂર જોશમાં કામ ચલાવી રહ્યા હોવાં છતાં પણ અંગ્રેજ સામ્રાજ્યશાહી હકુમતે તેને સરકારી રીતે નોંધવાની મના કરેલ. સંઘને તોડવાના પણ ઘણાં પ્રયત્નો કરવામાં આવ્યા. પરંતુ મજૂરોની એકતા તો વધતી જ ગઈ. જૂન-૧૯૩૫ અને જૂન ૧૯૩૭ દરમિયાન સંઘના સભ્યો ૪૮૦થી વધી ૨,૫૦૦ થયા. મજૂરોના આ જોર સામે સરકારને મે ૧૯૩૭માં સંઘને સરકારી દસ્તાવેજમાં નોંધવું પડ્યું.

મજૂર સંઘના કામને જાહેરાત આપવા માટે કસ્વાહીલી, પંજાબી, ગુજરાતી તેમ જ ઉર્દૂમાં ચોપાનિયા છપાવી ગામે ગામ વહેંચવામાં આવ્યા. ૧૯૩૬માં મખન સહિના તંત્રીપદ નીચે 'કેન્યા વર્કર' નામનું છાપું પંજાબી અને ઉર્દૂમાં મજૂર સંઘે બહાર પાડ્યું.

છેલ્લા બે વર્ષમાં કેન્યા મજૂર સંઘનું જોર એટલું બધું વધી ગયું હતું કે કેન્યાના ગામો ઉપરાંત યુગાન્ડા તેમ જ ટાંગાનિકા(ટાન્ઝાન્યા)માં પણ તેના સભ્યો હતા. એટલે માર્ચ ૧૯૩૭માં ફરી તેનું નામ બદલાવી પૂર્વ આફ્રિકા મજૂર સંઘ (લેબર ટ્રેડ યુનયિન ઓફ ઈસ્ટ આફ્રિકા) રાખવામાં આવ્યું.

૧૯૩૯ની સંઘની સભામાં મખન સહિ સાથે જેસી કરયુકી અને જ્યોર્જ ડેગવા પણ સંઘની સમિતિમાં ચૂંટાયા. આ સભામાં આફ્રિકી અને કેન્યાવાસી ભારતીય મજૂરોએ મોટી સંખ્યામાં ભાગ લીધેલો. સભામાં ભાષણો કસ્વાહીલી, હદિસ્તાની અને અંગ્રેજીમાં કરવામાં આવેલા.

મખન સહિ મજૂરોના હક્કની લડતની સાથે સાથે બીજી લડતોમાં પણ ભાગ લીધેલો. તેઓની નેતાગીરી હેઠળ મજૂર સંઘે ભારત, ચાઈના, પેલેસ્ટાઈન, ઈથિયોપિયા વગેરે દેશોની સ્વતંત્રતાની લડાઈઓને સાથ આપતા ઠરાવો પસાર કર્યા. તેઓએ કેન્યામાં સામ્રાજ્યશાહી સરકાર પાસે કોઈ પણ પૂરતબિંધ વગર બોલવાની, સભા બોલાવવાની, સંસ્થાઓ સંગઠિત કરવાની વગેરે છૂટો માટે પડકાર કરેલો.

મખન સહિ ઈસ્ટ આફ્રિકિન ઈન્ડયિન નેશનલ કોંગ્રેસ સમિતિના સભ્ય તેમ જ ઈન્ડયિન યુથ લીગના મંત્રી પણ હતા.

૧૯૪૦માં મખનસહિ ભારત ગયા. ત્યાં તેઓએ મજૂર સંઘોનો અભ્યાસ કર્યો અને ત્યાંની આઝાદીની લડતમાં ભાગ લીધો. અંગ્રેજ સામ્રાજ્ય સરકારે અમદાવાદમાં તેઓની

ધરપકડ કરી બે વર્ષના સમય સુધી અટકાયતી કેદમાં રાખ્યા. કેદમાં તેઓએ ૧૬૦ બીજા કેદીઓ સાથે મળી, કેદીઓ તરીકે પોતાના હકોની માંગ કરતાં ભૂખ હડતાળ કરી.

૧૯૪૨માં કેદમાંથી છૂટ્યા પછી પણ મખનસહિને પરદેશી સરકારે ઘરજખ નામના ગામડાની બહાર નીકળવાની મના કરી. તેઓ ત્યાં ૧૯૪૫ સુધી રહ્યા. ત્યાર બાદ તેઓએ સામ્યવાદી પક્ષનું છાપું 'જંગે આઝાદી'માં સહાયક તંત્રીનું કામ કર્યું.

ઓગષ્ટ ૧૯૪૭માં જ્યારે તેઓ પાછા કેન્યા આવ્યા તો તેઓને અંગ્રેજ સરકારે દેશ નકિલ કર્યા. આ હુકમ માનવાની તેઓએ ચોખ્ખી મના કરી અને અદાલતમાં હુકમનામા સામે લડી અને જીત્યા. ત્યાર બાદ તેઓ પાછા મજૂર સંઘ અને રાજનીતિના કામે પૂરજોશમાં લાગી પડ્યા.

જ્યારે ૧૯૪૮માં ગોરી સરકારે કેન્યાવાસી ભારતીઓમાં હદ્દિ-મુસલમાન ભેદભાવોને ઉત્તેજન આપ્યું ત્યારે મખન સહિ તે ચળવળની વિરૃદ્ધ ભૂખ હડતાલ કરી.

ઑક્ટોબર ૧૯૪૮માં અંગ્રેજ સરકારે મખનસહિની ધરપકડ કરી અને ફરી દેશ-નકિલ કરવાનો પ્રયત્ન કર્યો. પરંતુ બે અઠવાડિયા પછી પોતાની હાર માની તેઓને મુક્ત કર્યા.

૧૯૪૯માં જ્યારે આફ્રિકી અને કેન્યાવાસી એશિયન મજૂરોના નેતાઓએ સાથે મળી એક નવું કેન્દ્રરયિ સંઘ – ઇસ્ટ આફ્રિકિન ટ્રેડ યુનિયનસ કૉંગ્રેસ ઊભું કર્યું ત્યારે તેના પ્રમુખ તરીકે ફ્રેડ કુબાઈ અને મંત્રી તરીકે મખનસહિ ચૂંટાયા હતા.

૨૯ એપ્રિલ ૧૯૫૦ કેન્યા માટે એક ઐતિહાસિક દિવસ છે. આ દિવસે કલોવેની હોલ, નાઇરોબીમાં કેન્યા આફ્રિકિન યુનિયન અને ઇસ્ટ આફ્રિકિન ઇન્ડિયન કૉંગ્રેસના હસ્તકે એક સભા બોલાવવામાં આવેલી. આ સભામાં જે ઠરાવો પસાર થયા તેમાંનો એક ઠરાવ મખનસહિ પેશ કરેલો. તેમાં તેઓએ જોરદાર માંગણી કરી કે પૂર્વ આફ્રિકાના સર્વે મુલકોને સામ્રાજ્યશાહીના કબજામાંથી છૂટકારો મળવો જોઈએ અને કોઈ પણ શરત વગર અને ઢીલ વગર આઝાદી મળવી જોઈએ.

મખન સહિની મજૂરોના હક્કો અને દેશની આઝાદી માટેની લડત તેમ જ તેઓને આફ્રિકી અને કેન્યાવાસી એશિયન જનતાનો મળતો ટેકો, આ બધું જોઈ અને ગોરી સરકાર

ગભરાઈ ગઈ હતી. ૧૫ મે ૧૯૫૦ના દિવસે તેઓની ધરપકડ કરવામાં આવી. મખન સહિની સાથે ચેંગે કબિઆશ્યા અને ફ્રેડ કુબાઈની પણ ધરપકડ કરવામાં આવેલી. પોતાના નેતાઓને કેદ કરવામાં આવ્યા તેની વિરુદ્ધ આખા દેશના મજૂરોએ દસ દિવસ માટે હડતાલ કરેલી.

કોઈ પણ આરોપ વગર મખન સહિને કાયર સરકારે સાડા અગિયાર વર્ષ સુધી કેદમાં રાખ્યા. તેઓએ આ વર્ષો લોકીટીંગ, મારાલાલ અને ડોલ ડોલમાં ગુજાર્યા. આ હિમતવાન લડવૈયાની લડત તો કેદમાં પણ ચાલુ જ રહી.

૧૯૫૨માં દસ દિવસની, ૧૯૫૯માં ૧૨ દિવસની અને ૧૯૬૧માં ૨૧ દિવસની ભૂખ હડતાલ તેઓએ કરી. આ સાથે કેદખાના અને ડીટેન્શન કેમ્પોમાંથી પણ છૂપે રસ્તે પોતાના સાથીઓને અને સામ્રાજ્યશાહી સરકારને પડકાર કરતાં સંદેશાઓ તેઓએ મોકલવાનું ચાલુ રાખ્યું. ૧૯૫૨થી ૧૯૬૧ સુધી માઉ માઉની આઝાદીની લડાઈ પૂર જોશમાં ચાલી. છેલ્લે અંગ્રેજ સરકારે હતાશ થઈ આઝાદીના લડવૈયાઓને કેદમાંથી છોડવા પડ્યા. હજારો કેદીઓ છૂટ્યા તેમાં મખનસહિ પણ હતા. તેઓ ૨૨ ઑક્ટોબર ૧૯૬૧માં આઝાદ થયા.

કેદમાંથી નીકળ્યા બાદ મખનસહિ દેશ અને મજૂરોના હિત માટે લડવાનું ચાલુ રાખ્યું. આ સાથે કેન્યાના મજૂરોની લડતનો ઇતિહાસ પણ લખ્યો. ૧૯૬૯માં તેઓનું પુસ્તક 'હિસ્ટરી ઑફ કેન્યાઝ ટ્રેડ યુનિયન મુવમેન્ટ ટુ ૧૯૫૨' પ્રસિદ્ધ થયું અને ૧૯૮૦માં 'કેન્યાઝ ટ્રેડ યુનિયનસ, ૧૯૫૨-૧૯૫૬' પ્રગટ થયું. આ સિવાય તેઓએ કેન્યાની ઐતિહાસિક સંસ્થા (કેન્યા હિસ્ટોરીકલ એસોસિએશન)ની વાર્ષિક સભાઓમાં પણ અનેક લેખો રજૂ કર્યા.

મખન સહિનું મૃત્યુ ૬૩ વર્ષની ઉંમરે ૧૯૭૩માં થયું. તેઓની યાદી હંમેશ માટે કાયમ રહે તે માટે નાઇરોબીનો એક રસ્તો કે જે તેઓની જૂની નશિઆળ જામ્હૂરી હાઈ સ્કૂલની સામે છે તેનું નામ મખનસહિ રોડ રાખવામાં આવ્યું છે.

સૌજન્ય : "અલક મલક", દીવાળી અંક, નવેમ્બર ૧૯૮૫; પૃ. ૧૯-૨૧.

Makhan Singh (1913-1973)

Makhan Singh was born on 27 December, 1913 in Gharjak, a small village in Punjab (now in Pakistan). His father, Sudh Singh, was a carpenter who came to Kenya in 1920 and took up a job with the railways. Makhan Singh and his mother Ishar Kaur came to Kenya in 1927.

Sudh Singh, who was a member of the Railways Labour Union, had started a fight for their rights and was thus sacked from the job. He became self-employed by opening the Punjab Printing Press.

Makhan Singh studied at the Government Indian High School (now renamed Jamhuri High School) in Nairobi and passed the London Matriculation Examination in 1931. He was keen to study further but due to poor financial conditions of the family he could not continue his studies. He started working at the Punjab Printing Press. In 1934, he went to India, got married to Satwant Kaur and returned to Kenya.

Makhan Singh took interest in the world of politics and labour–peasant movement at an early age. He wrote poems in the Punjabi language about the fight against imperialism in Kenya and India and recited these at public gatherings.

In 1935, Makhan Singh was elected as the Secretary of Kenya Indian Trade Union. He, along with his comrades, had realised that the workers needed unity to protect their interests. The imperialist government tried to divide Indian and African workers. In order to overcome racial division, the Indian Workers

Union changed its name to Labour Trade Union of Kenya. Its membership was open to all. Makhan Singh was elected as Secretary of this new union as well.

Under his leadership, trade unions achieved great success. As a result of union agitation and struggle against the Railways, the company was in 1935

forced to permanently employ its many employees who had worked as casual labourers for years.

In April – May 1937, the Trade Union declared a strike to demand an increase in salaries of the factory workers in Nairobi. This was a success and the factory owners were compelled to raise the salaries by 15 – 25%.

This Trade Union was fully active and yet the imperialist British Government had refused to register it. Many attempts were made to break the union, but the unity among workers grew stronger. Between June 1935 and June 1937, the membership increased from 480 to 2,500. As a result, the government had to recognise and register the union in 1937.

To give publicity to the Trade Union's activities, leaflets were printed and distributed in Kiswahili, Punjabi, Gujarati and Urdu. In 1936, the Trade Union published the newsletter *Kenya*

Worker in Punjabi and Urdu under the editorship of Makhan Singh.

During the last two years the Trade Union of Kenya had become so strong that apart from towns in Kenya, it also had members in Uganda and Tanganyika (Tanzania). Therefore, in March 1937, it was renamed Labour Trade Union of East Africa.

In 1939, along with Makhan Singh, J. C. Kariuki and George Ndegwa also got elected to the Union's committee. A large number of African and Indian Kenya workers were present at this meeting. The speeches were made in Kiswahili, Hindustani and English languages.

Apart from the fight for workers' rights, Makhan Singh took part in other struggles as well. Under his leadership the Trade Union passed resolutions supporting the freedom movements of India, China, Palestine, Ethiopia among others. They demanded from the imperialist government of Kenya the right to free speech, assembly and freedom to form organisations without any restrictions.

Makhan Singh was also a committee member of the East African Indian National Congress and Secretary of the Indian Youth League.

In 1940, Makhan Singh went to India where he studied the trade union movement and participated in the freedom struggle. The British Government arrested him in Ahmedabad and imprisoned him for two years. While in prison, he went on a hunger strike demanding rights as a prisoner.

In 1942, after he was released from prison, the colonial government forbade him from going out of Dharjakh village. He was confined there until 1945. Thereafter he worked as associate editor of the communist party's newsletter *Jang-e- Azadi* [Freedom Struggle].

In August 1947 when he returned to Kenya, the British Government issued an order for his exile which he refused to obey. He challenged it in the court and won the case. After this victory, he once again resumed his mission of trade unionism and politics.

In 1948, when the British Government conspired to divide the Indian Kenyan Hindus and Muslims, Makhan Singh went on a hunger strike to oppose this.

In October 1948, the British Government arrested Makhan Singh again and attempted to banish him from the country. But after two weeks, it backtracked and released him.

In 1949, African and Asian Kenyan workers organised a new umbrella organisation called East Africa Trade Unions Congress. Fred Kubai was elected President and Makhan Singh its Secretary.

29 April 1950 is a historical day for Kenya. On that day a meeting was held under the joint auspices of Kenya African Union and East African Indian Congress at Kaloleni Hall in Nairobi. One of the resolutions passed at this meeting was proposed by Makhan Singh. In this proposal he strongly demanded that all the East African countries must be freed from the clutches of imperialism and given unconditional independence without delay.

Makhan Singh's fight for workers' rights and the support he had from the African and Asian Kenyans people had made the British Government nervous. He was arrested on 15th May 1950. Others arrested with him were Chege Kibacia and Fred Kubai. Workers all over the country went on strike for ten days in protest.

Makhan Singh was kept in prison for eleven and a half years without any charge by the dastardly government. He spent these years in Lokitaung, Maralal and Doldol. This brave fighter continued his struggle even in prison. He went on a hunger strike for 10 days in 1952, for 12 days in 1959 and for 21 days in 1961. From within prison and detention camp walls, he continued to send to his comrades secret messages of resistance against the imperialist government.

The Mau Mau freedom struggle was in full swing from 1952 to 1961. Finally, the British Government had to release the freedom fighters from prison. Makhan Singh was one of them. He was freed on 22nd October 1961.

After his release from prison Makhan Singh continued to fight for workers' interests. He also wrote a history of Kenya's trade union movement. His book *History of Kenya's Trade Union Movements to 1952* was published in 1969. In addition, he presented several papers of the annual meetings of Kenya's Historical Association.

Makhan Singh passed away in 1976 at the age of 63. The second volume of his history of the trade union movement Kenya, *Kenya's Trade Unions, 1952 – 1956* was published posthumously in 1980. The road in front of his alma mater Jamhuri High School in Nairobi has been named Makhan Singh Road to keep his memory alive.

Alakmalak, November 1985.

અંબુભાઈ પટેલ (૧૯૧૯-૧૯૭૭)

દેશપ્રેમી એશિયન કેન્યાવાસીઓનાં જીવન ચરિત્ર - 1 — 5

દેશપ્રેમી એશિયન કે-ન્યાવાસીઓનાં જીવન ચરિત્ર - 1

અંબુભાઇ પટેલ

અંબુભાઇ પટેલનો જન્મ 1919માં ગુજરાતના ભાદરણ ગામમાં થયો હતો. નાની ઉંમરથી તેઓએ ભારતની આઝાદીની લડતમાં ભાગ લીધેલો. 14 વરસની ઉંમરે તેઓએ જેલની યાત્રા કરેલી. ત્યાર બાદ બીજી બે વખત અંગ્રેજ સામ્રાજ્યશાહીઓએ તેઓની ધરપકડ કરી જેલ ભેગા ય કરેલા.

12-13 વરસની વયે તેઓએ એક ફોટોગ્રાફર સાથે સ્વતંત્રતા આંદોલનનું કામ શરૂ કર્યું. ગુજરાતમાં જ્યાં જ્યાં દેશપ્રેમીઓ હડતાલ પાડે, મોરચાઓ કાઢે અને ત્યાં પરદેશી પોલીસ ફોજીઓ તેઓ ઉપર ક્રૂરતાથી લાઠીમાર કરે ત્યારે છુપાઈને તેઓના ફોટા પાડી દેશભરના અખબારોને પહોંચાડે.

અંબુભાઈએ ગાંધીજીના સાબરમતી આશ્રમમાં ત્રણ વર્ષ ગાળ્યા અને ત્યાં બીમારોની સેવા કરી. ત્યાર બાદ જ્યારે ગાયકવાડના મુસલમાન કાગળ બન-વનારાઓએ ગાંધીજી-ના કહેવા પર એક શાળા શરૂ કરી, ત્યારે તેઓએ ત્યાં બે વરસ કાગળ બન-વવાનો અને ચોપડી બાંધવાનો અભ્યાસક્રમ કર્યો.

1943માં તેઓના લગ્ન પૂર્વ આફ્રિકાના રહેવાસી બીલાબહેન સાથે થયા. લગ્ન બાદ તેઓ થોડો વખત યુગા-ડા રહેવા ગયા અને 1946માં -ૈરોબી આવ્યા. ભારતની સાથે લઇ આવેલી ચોપડીઓ તેઓએ રસ્તામાં જકાત રહી ત્યારે તો ઘરે વેચી પોતાનું ગુજરાન ચલાવ્યું. થોડા વખત પછી 'જય હિંદ' બુકશોપ ખોલી.

1948માં ભારતના કેન-ય ખાતેના એલ્ચીથી, આપ પંત સાથે મળી ક્યામ્પ્ખુ-ના જિંજામાં એક ક્રાંતા અને કાપડ વણવાની શાળા ખોલી. ઉકામ્પ-ની- માં પાણી-ની અછત દૂર કરવા તેઓએ ત્યાંના ખેડૂતો સાથે મળી કુવાઓ ખોદ્યા, જે આજે પણ ત્યાંની વસ્તીને પાણી પૂરૂં પાડે છે.

અંબુભાઈ પટેલનો જન્મ ૧૯૧૯માં ગુજરાતના ભાદરણ ગામમાં થયો હતો. નાની ઉંમરથી તેઓએ ભારતની આઝાદીની લડતમાં ભાગ લીધેલો. ૧૪ વરસની ઉંમરે તેઓએ જેલની યાત્રા કરેલી. તૂયાર બાદ બીજી બે વખત અંગ્રેજી સામ્રાજ્યશાહીઓ એ તેઓની ધરપકડ કરી જેલ ભેગા ય કરેલા.

૧૨-૧૩ વરસની વયે તેઓએ એક ફોટોગ્રાફર સાથે સ્વતંત્રતા આંદોલનનું કામ શરૂ કર્યું. ગુજરાતમાં જ્યાં જ્યાં દેશપૂરેમીઓ હડતાલ પાડે, મોરચાઓ કાઢે અને તૂયાં પરદેશી પોલીસ ફોજીઓ તેઓ ઉપર ક્રૂરતાથી લાઠીમાર કરે તૂયારે છુપાઈને તેઓના ફોટા પાડી દેશભરના અખબારોને પહોંચાડે.

અંબુભાઈએ ગાંધીજીના સાબરમતી આશ્રમમાં તૂરણ વરૂષ ગાળ્યા અને તૂયાં બીમારોની સેવા કરી. તૂયાર બાદ જ્યારે ગાયકવાડના મુસલમાન કાગળ બનાવનારાઓએ ગાંધીજીના કહેવા પર એક શાળા શરૂ કરી, તૂયારે તેઓએ તૂયાં બે વરસ કાગળ બનાવવાનો અને ચોપડી બાંધવાનો

અભ્યાસક્રમ કર્યો.

૧૯૪૩માં તેઓના લગ્ન પૂર્વ આફ્રિકાના રહેવાસી લીલાબહેન સાથે થયા. લગ્ન બાદ તેઓ થોડો વખત યુગાન્ડા રહેવા ગયા અને ૧૯૪૬માં નાઈરોબી આવ્યા. ભારતથી સાથે લઈ આવેલી ચોપડીઓ તેઓએ રસ્તામાં ઊભા રહી અથવા તો ઘરે ઘરે જઈ વેચી પોતાનું ગુજરાન ચલાવ્યું. થોડા વખત પછી 'જય હિંદ બુકશોપ' ખોલી.

૧૯૪૮માં ભારતના કેન્યા ખાતેના એલ્ચી, આપા પંત સાથે મળી ક્યામ્બુના જલિલામાં એક કાંતવા અને કાપડ વણવાની શાળા ખોલી. ઉકામ્બાનીમાં પાણીની અછત દૂર કરવા તેઓએ ત્યાંના ખેડૂતો સાથે મળી કૂવાઓ ખોદ્યા, જે આજે પણ ત્યાંની વસ્તીને પાણી પૂરું પાડે છે.

ભારતની આઝાદીની લડતનો અનુભવ ધરાવતા અંબુભાઈએ કેન્યાની સ્વતંત્રતા માટે લડી રહેલા આફ્રિકનો સાથે મળી આ લડતમાં પૂરેપૂરો ભાગ લીધો. કેન્યા આફ્રિકન યુનિયનના નેતાઓ (જેવા કે, મ્ઝે જોમો કેન્યાટા, મ્બીયુ કોઈનાંગે, આચીયેંગ ઓનેકો, વગેરે) અને સામાન્ય સભ્યો સાથે ભળીને કામ કર્યું. સામ્રાજ્યશાહી વિરોધી આંદોલનમાં બીજા એશિયન કેન્યાવાસીઓ જેવા કે મખનસિંહ, પીઓ ગામા પીટો, ગિરધારીલાલ વિદ્યાર્થી સાથે તેઓએ ભળી આ લડત આગળ ચલાવી.

૧૯૫૨માં જ્યારે આઝાદીની હથિયારબંધ લડાઈ શરૂ થઈ, ત્યારે તેઓએ હથિયાર, અનાજ, કપડાં તેમ જ પૈસા ભેગા કરી માઉ માઉ આંદોલનના સ્વતંત્રતાના સૈનિકોને લડાઈના ઈલાકામાં મોકલવાનો બંદોબસ્ત કર્યો. ઘણીવાર તેઓએ લડવૈયાઓને અંગ્રેજી પોલીસ અને લશ્કરના પંજામાંથી બચાવવા પોતાના ઘરમાં અથવા તો દુકાનમાં છુપાવ્યા. અંગ્રેજી પોલીસે અનેક વખત તેઓના ઘરની અને દુકાનની તલાશી લીધી પણ એકદમ કાળજી રાખવાવાળા અંબુભાઈએ તેઓના હાથમાં કાંઈ પણ પુરાવો ન આવવા દીધો.

ઘણીવાર એવું પણ બન્યું કે કોઈ માઉ માઉના લડવૈયાઓ ઘરમાં હોય અને પોલીસની ધાડ પડે. ઘરના પાછળના ભાગમાં તેઓ કોલસાની ગુણીઓ રાખતા, જલ્દીથી તેઓ આ લડવૈયાઓને આ ગુણીમાં સંતાડી દે. તપાસ લેતાં ફિરંગી પોલીસને કાંઈ જ ન મળતાં નિરાશ થઈ પાછું જાવું પડે.

કેપેનગુરયાનો મુકદમો કે જેમાં જોમો કેન્યાટા, આચીયેંગ ઓનેકો, બીલ્દાદ કાગીઆ, થુંબું કરૂમ્બા અને પોલ નગેને ખોટા આક્ષેપ ઉપર જેલની સજા થયેલી. કેસ જ્યારે પૂરો થયો ત્યારે સરકારે અદાલતનો ચુકાદો જાહેર કરવાની મના કરી. અંબુભાઈ અને પીટોએ ભેગા મળી આ ચુકાદાને આમ જનતા અને આંતરરાષ્ટ્રીય જનતા સમક્ષ પેશ કરવાની એક છૂપી યોજના તૈયાર

કરી. આ ૧૦૦ પત્રતાના ચુકાદાની ગુપ્ત રીતે 300 નકલો છાપી. ૨૫૦ નકલોને ટપાલ દ્વારા અનેક દેશોના નેતાઓને અંગ્રેજી સરકારના જ કવરમાં નાખી મોકલ્યા. બીજી ૫૦ નકલોની વહેંચણી છૂપી રીતે દેશમાં કરી. આવી રીતે દુનિયાને આ બેઇનૂસાફી અને બનિપાયેદાર મુકદ્દમા વશિ જાણ થઈ.

આ કટોકટીના સમય દરમિયાન દેશની હાલત વશિના સર્વ સમાચાર અંગ્રેજી સામ્રાજ્યશાહી સરકાર મારફત નીકળતા એટલે તે એકપક્ષી હતા. આવા ખોટા સમાચારનો વિરોધ કરતા અને દેશની જનતાને લડાઈના બારામાં સાચા ખબર પહોંચાડવામાં અંબુભાઈએ નાઇરોબીના માઉ માઉના અનેક લડવૈયાઓના ફોટા પાડી, તેઓએ શહીદી વહોરી લીધી. ત્યારબાદ તેઓની યાદી તાજી રાખવાનું શક્ય કર્યું. જ્યારે મોતને આંગણે આવા લડવૈયાઓ ઊભા હોય અને તેઓના સામ્રાજ્યશાહીઓની અદાલતોમાં મુકદ્દમા ચાલતા હોય, ત્યારે અંબુભાઈ પોતાનો કેમેરો લઈ અદાલતમાં પહોંચી જાય. ન્યેરીમાં ૧૯૫૭માં જ્યારે ફ્લિડ માર્શલ ઉડાન કીમાથીનો મુકદ્દમો ચાલી રહ્યો હતો ત્યારે આઝાદીની લડતના આ મશહુર નેતાનો ફોટો તેઓએ પાડેલો. આ ફોટો હજી સુધી દેશના અનેક ગામના રસ્તે રસ્તે વેચાઈ રહ્યો છે અને અનેક કેન્યાવાસીઓના ઘરે જોવા મળે છે.

૧૯૫૫-૧૯૬૩ દરમિયાન એક બાજુ આઝાદીની લડત હથિયાર સાથે ચાલી રહી હતી, બીજી તરફ હતી કાયદેસરની લડત. આ લડતના વડાઓમાં આફ્રિકિ નેતાઓ ઓગીન્ગા ઓડીન્ગા, ટોમ મ્બોયા વગેરે, અને એશયિન કેન્યાવાસીઓ કે. પી. શાહ, ચનન સહિ વગેરેનો સમાવેશ હતો. આ લડતમાં પણ અંબુભાઈએ પાછી પાની ના કરી અને આ બીજા નેતાઓ સાથે મળી રાજકીય આંદોલનને સફળ બનાવવામાં અનેક ભોગ આપ્યા..

૧૯૬૦-૬૧ દરમ્યાન અંબુભાઈએ એક નવી ઝુંબેશ ઉપાડી : કોઈ પણ કાનૂની કાર્યવાહી વગર અંગ્રેજ સરકારે હજારો કેન્યાના નાગરિકોને કેદમાં રાખેલ તેઓની મુક્તિ ઝુંબેશ. આ કામ માટે દેશપુરેમી કેન્યાવાસી એશયિનો પાસેથી પૈસા એકઠા કર્યા. દેશ દેશના નેતાઓને કાગળ દ્વારા અરજી કરી કે તેઓ અંગ્રેજ સરકારને દબાણ કરે. કેદીઓની મુક્તિની માંગનો પડકાર કરતાં ભીંતપત્રો છપાવી રસ્તે રસ્તે ચોંટાડ્યા. મુક્તિની માંગ કરતાં પત્રો પર હજારો સહીઓ એકઠી કરી અનેક મોરચા રચ્યા..

આઝાદીના આ બધા કામમાં અંબુભાઈને લીલાબહેનનો પૂરેપૂરો સાથ હતો. બંનેને આ લડતમાં કોઈપણ જાતનો અંગત સ્વાર્થ ન હતો. દેશની સ્વતંત્રતા અને આમ જનતાના હિતમાં કામ કરવું એ જ તેમનો ઉપદેશ અને તે જ તેઓનો ધર્મ. જો તેઓ ઇચ્છતા હોત તો ઘણી મૂડી કમાઈ શકત, પરંતુ તે માટે પોતાના નિઃસ્વાર્થ સદ્ધિાંતો અને દેશભક્તિની લડત છોડવી પડત.

આમ કરવા આ દેશપ્રેમી જોડી જરા ય તૈયાર નહતી. એટલે જ આખી જંદિગી તેઓએ ગરીબીમાં કાઢી.

૧૯૬૦માં કેન્યાને સ્વતંત્રતા મળતાં અંબુભાઈ પાછાં પોતાના ચોપડી બાંધવાના ધંધામાં લાગી ગયા. તે સાથે દેશના ઇતિહાસ વિશે ચોપડીઓ, છાપાંનાં લખાણો અને ફોટાઓ (ઓક્ટોબર ૧૯૬૨માં કટોકટીના સમયને શરૂ થયાને દસ વરસના પ્રસંગે અંબુભાઈએ ૧૮૯૦થી ચાલુ થયેલો સામ્રાજ્યશાહી વિરુદ્ધની લડાઈના જે પોતાની પાસે ફોટાઓનો સંગ્રહ હતો તેનું એક ભવ્ય પ્રદર્શન યોજ્યું.) ભેગા કરવાનો જે પહેલેથી શોખ હતો તે માટે હવે તેઓએ વધારે વખ્ત આપ્યો. આ સાથે ઐતિહાસિક લખાણ લખવાનું પણ ચાલુ રાખ્યું.

૧૯૫૪-૫૫ દરમ્યાન તેઓએ જોમો કેન્યાટાની 'માય પીપલ ઑફ કીકુયુ' અને 'કેન્યાઝ સ્ટ્રગલ ફોર ફ્રીડમ'નો તરજુમો ગુજરાતીમાં કર્યો. તેઓએ ન્યુ કેન્યા પબ્લિશિર્સ નામ હેઠળ પ્રકાશકનું કામ શરૂ કર્યું. અને 'જોમો ધી ગ્રેટ' અને ૧૨ ડિસેમ્બર ૧૯૬૦ એટલે કે આઝાદીના જ દિવસે, 'સ્ટ્રગલ ફોર રીલીઝ જોમો કેન્યાટા એન્ડ હીઝ કલીગ્ઝ' નામનાં પુસ્તકો બહાર પાડ્યા. ત્યાર બાદ 'એડીન્ગા ઇન ઇન્ડિયા' અને પીટોના દુઃખદ મૃત્યુ બાદ 'પીઓ ગામા પીન્ટો', 'ઇન્ડપિન્ડન્ટ કેન્યાઝ ફર્સ્ટ માર્ટીર' બહાર પાડ્યા.

અંબુભાઈને કવિતા લખવાનો પણ શોખ હતો. તેઓએ એક કવિતા કિસ્વાહિલી અને કીકુયુ ભાષાઓમાં કીમાથી અને બીજા આઝાદીના શૂરવીરોની શાનમાં લખેલ. આ કવિતા તેઓ એક ગુજરાતી ગીતના રાગમાં ગાતા. એક વખત બીબીસીના એક ખબરપત્રીએ આનું રેકોર્ડિંગ કરેલ અને પછી રેડિયો દ્વારા આખી દુનિયામાં પ્રસારિત કર્યું.

અંબુભાઈનાં છપાયેલાં લખાણો સિવાય તેઓએ એમ. એ. દેસાઈ, એ. એમ. જીવનજી, મખનસિંહ, ઓગીન્ગા ઓડીન્ગા, ટોમ મ્બોયાની આત્મકથાઓ પ્રગટ કરવા માટે તૈયાર કરેલ. સેંકડો માઉ માઉના લડવૈયાના જે ફોટો તેઓએ એકઠા કર્યા હતા તેને પણ ચોપડીના રૂપમાં છપાવવાનો તેઓનો ઇરાદો હતો.

પરંતુ આ બધું કામ પૂરું થાય તે પહેલાં આ દેશપ્રેમીનું હૃદયરોગને કારણે ૫૮ વર્ષની ઉંમરે નાઇરોબીમાં ડિસેમ્બર ૧૯૭૭માં દુઃખદ અવસાન થયું. આવા દેશપ્રેમીઓના જીવનમાંથી આપણે પણ આપણાં જીવનમાં કાંઇક સદ્‌કાર્ય – દેશભક્તિનો ગુણ ઉતારીએ અને તેઓના અધૂરાં રહેલાં કાર્યોને પૂરણ કરવા પ્રયત્નો કરીએ તો ....

સૌજન્ય : "અલકમલક", ઓક્ટોબર ૧૯૮૫; પૃ. ૨૬-૨૮.

Ambubhai Patel (1919-1977)

Ambubhai Patel was born in Bhadran in the state of Gujarat, India. He joined the freedom movement when he was still young and was sent to prison at the age of 14. Thereafter the British imperialists arrested and imprisoned him twice.

He became a freedom fighter at the tender age of twelve or thirteen along with a photographer friend. They secretly took photographs of protesters and marchers being mercilessly lathicharged, caned, by the police and sent them to newspapers all over the country.

Ambubhai was an inmate at Gandhiji's Sabarmati Ashram for three years where he tended the sick. At Gandhiji's behest, the Muslim paper manufacturers of Gaikawad had opened a training institute. Ambubhai joined it and trained as a paper maker and book binder for two years.

He was married to Leelaben of East Africa in 1943. After marriage he lived in Uganda for some time and then moved to Nairobi in 1946. He earned his livelihood by selling the books he had brought from India. Initially he did this as a vendor and later, opened the Jai Hind Bookshop.

In 1948, in collaboration with Apa Pant, the then ambassador of India, he opened a spinning and weaving centre in Kiambu district. There was acute water shortage in Ukambani and so with the help of local farmers, he dug three wells which supply water to date.

Utilising his experience as a freedom fighter in India, Ambubhai took active part in the freedom struggle of Kenya. He worked with the Kenya African Union leaders such as Jomo Kenyatta, Mbiyu Koinange, and Achieng' Oneko among others, as well as the common members of the public. He joined the other Asian Kenyans such as Makhan Singh, Pio Gama Pinto and Girdharilal Vidyarthi in their struggle against imperialism.

In 1952 when the armed struggle for freedom started, he would collect arms, food grains, clothes and money and send them to the Mau Mau freedom fighters. He often gave them shelter in his house or shop to keep them safe from the prying eyes of the British police and army. On many occasions, the British police raided his house and shop but he was careful enough not to leave any evidence for them.

Quite often it so happened that the raids took place when the Mau Mau freedom fighters were in the house. Ambubhai used to store sacks of coal in the backyard of his house so he would quickly hide the freedom fighters in these sacks and the police would leave disappointed.

When the Kapenguria trial in which Kenyatta, Achieng Oneko, Bildad Kaggia, Kungu Karumba and Paul Ngei were sentenced to prison on false charges was over, the government ordered the decision not to be made public. But Ambubhai and Pinto prepared a secret plan to leak this to the general public and international agencies. They printed 300 copies of this 100-page judgement.

They posted 250 copies to the leaders of various countries using the British Government's envelops. The remaining 50 copies were distributed inside the country. Thus the world came to know about this unjust and unfounded trial.

During this period of emergency, all news came out through the British imperialist government. It was therefore never a surprise that it was always one-sided. To counter the biased and distorted news and to give the correct information regarding the freedom movement to the countrymen, Ambubhai took photographs of Mau Mau fighters and thus kept their memory alive after they were martyred. When the freedom fighters were being tried and were facing death penalty, Ambubhai went to the court with his camera. He is the one who took that iconic photograph of Field Marshal Dedan Kimathi in 1957 in Nyeri during his trial. This famous photograph is still being sold all over the country and is displayed in many Kenyan houses.

During 1955-1963, the armed struggle and civil movement for freedom were going on simultaneously. The leaders of this struggle included Africans such as Oginga Odinga, Tom Mboya and others, and Asian Kenyans like K. P. Shah, Chanan Singh to name but a few. In this struggle too, Ambubhai did not lag behind and participated fully to make it a success.

In 1960-61, Ambubhai started a new movement: a struggle for the release of thousands of Kenyan civilians imprisoned by the British government without a legal procedure. He raised funds for this from patriotic Asian Kenyans, wrote letters to world leaders requesting them to exert pressure on the British Government, displayed posters demanding the release of the prisoners, obtained thousands of signatures on the petition and organised protest marches.

Leelaben fully supported Ambubhai in all these activities. Their participation in this movement was selfless. Their aim was freedom of the country and welfare of its people. They had opportunities to make money and get rich, but they did not want to amass wealth at the cost of their principles and patriotic work. They refused to compromise and remained poor throughout their life. In 1963, when Kenya got freedom, Ambubhai once again resumed his trade of book binding. He now devoted more time to writing books about the history of Kenya as well as newspaper articles. He was also an avid photograph collector. To mark the tenth anniversary of the declaration of the state of emergency in Kenya, he organised a grand photographic exhibition in October 1962 that depicted the history of the freedom struggle since 1890. Collecting photographs was a hobby that he pursued passionately even as he continued writing historical articles.

In 1954-55, he translated into Gujarati Jomo Kenyatta's *My People of Gikuyu* and *Kenya's Struggle for Freedom*. He also founded the New Kenya Publishers firm and published *Jomo the Great*. On 12th December 1963, Kenya's Independence Day, he released *Struggle for Release of Jomo Kenyatta and his Colleagues*. Later, he published *Odinga in India*.This was to be followed by *Pio Gama Pinto, Independence Kenya's First Martyr*, a book that was published upon Pinto's death.

Ambubhai had a poetic mind too. He wrote a poem in Kiswahili and Kikuyu glorifying Kimathi and other brave freedom fighters. He used to sing this in a Gujarati rhythm. A BBC reporter recorded this and it was broadcast through radio the world over.

In addition to his published works, Ambubhai had prepared biographies of M. A. Desai, A. M. Jeevanjee, Makhan Singh, Oginga Odinga and Tom Mboya for publication. He had also intended to print the album of the photographs of Mau Mau fighters which he had collected and preserved. But these plans did not materialise as he died of a heart attack in December 1977 in Nairobi at the age of 58. His life is an inspiration to lovers of freedom everywhere.

Alakmalak October 1985.

પીઓ ગામા પીનૂટો (૧૯૨૭ - ૧૯૬૫)

પીઓ ગામા પીટો નો જન્મ નાઇરોબીમાં ૩૧ માર્ચ ૧૯૨૭માં થયો હતો. નાની ઉંમરમાં જ પતિઓ તેઓને ભારત ભણતર માટે મોકલ્યા હતા. ભણતર પૂરું કર્યા પછી થોડો વખત મુંબઈની પોસ્ટ એન્ડ ટેલિકોમ્યુનિકેશન કંપનીમાં કામ કર્યું. ત્યાં મજૂર સંઘના કામમાં ભાગ લઈ અને મજૂરોના હકો માટે હડતાલમાં ભાગ લીધો.

ગોવાની આઝાદી માટે પોર્ટુગીઝ સામ્રાજ્યશાહી વિરુદ્ધી ઝુંબેશમાં જોરદાર કામ કર્યું અને તે માટે છૂપે રસ્તે ગોવામાં દાખલ થયા. સામ્રાજ્ય સરકારે ગરિફ્તારીનો હુકમ બહાર પાડ્યો, પરંતુ બીજા આઝાદીના લડવૈયાઓની મદદથી તેઓ બહાર નીકળી ગયા અને ૧૯૪૯માં પાછા કેન્યા આવ્યા.

નાઇરોબીમાં પાછા આવ્યા પછી પીટોએ કાર્કુનનું કામ કર્યું પણ અંગ્રેજી સામ્રાજ્યશાહી નીચે દેશની ખરાબ હાલત જોતા સ્વતંત્રતાની લડત તરફ ખેંચાયા. ૧૯૫૧માં

ઇસ્ટ આફ્રિકિન ઇન્ડયિન કૉંગ્રેસની ક્ચેરી કે જે દેસાઈ મેમોરયિલ બલ્ડિગિમાં હતી ત્યાં કામે લાગ્યા. તેઓએ આફ્રિકી આઝાદી સંઘ, કેન્યા આફ્રિકિન યુનયિન, તેમ જ મજૂર સંઘોના સભ્યો અને નેતાઓ સાથે સંપર્ક સાધ્યો અને આફ્રિકી-એશયિન એકતા માટે કામ કર્યું. ૧૯૫૦માં જ્યારે મજૂરોના નેતા ચેંગે કબિાશ્યા, મખનસહિ અને ફ્રેડ કુબાઈની ધરપકડ કરવામાં આવી ત્યારે પીટો એ મજૂરો સાથે મળી, સંઘનું કામ ચાલુ રાખવામાં મદદ કરી.

આ બધું કામ સરળ રીતે થાય તે માટે તેઓએ કસ્વિાહીલી ભાષાનો અભ્યાસ કર્યો. આફ્રિકી જનતા સાથે ભળીને કામ કરવા માટે આ ભાષા શીખવી જ જોઈએ તેમ તેમને લાગ્યું.

અંગ્રેજી સામ્રાજ્યશાહી પ્રચારનો સામનો કરવા માટે તેઓએ પત્રકારત્વનું કામ ઉપાડ્યું. કોંકણી ભાષાના 'ઉઝ્વાદ' નામના ખબરપત્રના તંત્રી બન્યા. 'કોલોનયિલ ટાઇમ્સ'માં લખાણ લખ્યા, અને ૧૯૫૩માં ગુજરાતી-અંગ્રેજી 'ડેઇલી ક્રોનકિલ'નું તંત્રીપણું પીટોએ સ્વીકાર્યું. ડી. કે. શારદા, હારુન અહમ્મદ અને પૂરાણલાલ શેઠના સહકારથી અનેક અંગ્રેજી સરકાર વિરોધી આફ્રિકી ખબરપત્રોને છપાવવામાં મદદ કરી.

૨૦ ઓક્ટોબર ૧૯૫૨માં આઝાદીના સૈનકિો અને સામ્રાજ્યશાહીની ફોજ વચ્ચે જોરદાર લડાઈ શરૂ થઈ. અનેક આફ્રિકી નેતાઓ તેમ જ હજારો જનતાના માણસોને જેલો અને ડીટેન્શન કેમ્પોમાં ધકેલી દેવામાં આવ્યા. ઘણા દેશપ્રેમીઓની જમીન પરદેશી સરકારે જપ્ત કરી. બનિ ગુનેગાર આમ જનતા ઉપર જુલમ થવા લાગ્યા. આવા ક્રૂરતા ભરેલા કાયર સરકારના કામને પૂરસદ્ધિ કરવાનું કામ પીટો તેમ જ બીજા દેશપ્રેમીઓએ જેવા કે અંબુભાઈ પટેલે ઉપાડ્યું.

જે લડવૈયાઓને અદાલતમાં લઈ જવામાં આવ્યા તેઓ માટે વકીલો શોધવાનું કામ પણ

પીટોએ કર્યું. સરકાર સામે લડી આઝાદીના સૈનકિનો બચાવ કરવા માટે ઘણા દેશપ્રેમી એશયિન કેન્યાવાસીઓ આગળ આવ્યા. દા.ત. એફ. આર. ડીસુઝા, જે. એમ. નાઝારેથ, ઈ. કે. નવરોજી, એ. આર. કપીલા, એસ. એમ. અક્રમ, એ. એચ. મલીક, શેખ અમીન, કે. ડી. તુરવાડી, અરવદિ જમીનદાર વગેરે.

આ બધાં કામ સાથે માઉ માઉના લડવૈયાઓને હથિયારો અને બીજી જરૂરયિાતની ચીજો લડાઈના ઈલાકાઓમાં મોકલવાની સગવડ બીજા હમ્મિતવાન દેશપ્રેમીઓ સાથે મળીને કરી.

દેશની આઝાદી માટે આ બધુ કામ કર્યું તે ગોરી સરકારને ખટક્યું. ૧૯ જૂન ૧૯૫૪માં પીટોની ધરપકડ કરવામાં આવી અને માંડા ટાપુમાં ટાકવા ડીટેન્શન કેમ્પમાં કેદ રાખવામાં આવ્યા.

ધરપકડના ખાલી પાંચ મહિના પહેલાં તેઓના લગ્ન એમા સાથે થયા હતા.

માંડામાં બીજા ૨૦૦ દેશપ્રેમી કેદીઓ હતા જેમાં આચગ્બિંગ ઓનેકો, મુઇનૂગા ચોકવે અને જે. ડી. કાલીનો સમાવેશ હતો. પીટોએ તેઓ સાથે મળી સર્વે કેદીઓમાં એકતા રહે તેવું કામ કર્યું. સરકારે કેદીઓમાં અંદર અંદર ખટપટ ઊભી કરવાની અને ખોટી વાતો ફેલાવવાનો પ્રયત્ન કરેલ કે જેનાથી જેનાથી કેદીઓ આઝાદીની લડત છોડી દે. આ કોશિશની સામે પીટો અને બીજા આગેવાનોએ આ આઝાદીની લડતને ઉત્તેજન આપતા, મોઢેથી વાત ફેલાવતા એવા 'ખબરપત્રો' શરૂ કર્યા કે જેનાથી કેદીઓનો ઉત્સાહ વધ્યો. પીટો જ્યારે ડીટેન્શનમાં હતા ત્યારે તેઓના પતિનું અવસાન થયું. મરણ પથારીએથી પતિએ પુત્રને છેલ્લીવાર મળવાની અરજી સરકારને કરી પરંતુ દયાહીન સરકાર કે જેના માટે તેઓએ ૩૦ વરસ સુધી વફાદારીથી કામ કરેલ, એ સરકારે ચોખ્ખી ના પાડી દીધી. પતિનું મોત પુત્રને જોયા વગર જ થયું.

પીટો ૧૯૫૪-૧૯૫૭ દરમ્યાન માંડામાં અને ૧૯૫૮થી ૧૯૫૯ સુધી કાર્બાનેટમાં કેદ રહ્યા અને જુલાઈ ૧૯૫૯માં મુક્ત થયા. મુક્તિ બાદ તેઓના બીજા સાથીઓ જેઓ હજી કેદ ભોગવી રહ્યા હતા તેઓ તેમ જ તેઓના કુટુંબીઓ માટે પૈસા અને બીજી જરૂરિયાતની વસ્તુઓ એકઠી કરવાનું કામ કર્યું. કેદીઓ તેમ જ બીજા લડવૈયાઓના કુટુંબીઓ બીમાર હોય અને સારવાર કરાવવા માટે પૈસા ના હોય તેઓના મફત ઈલાજ માટે ઘણા એશિયન કેન્યાવાસી ડૉક્ટરો જેવા કે યુસુફ ઈરાજ વગેરે સાથે સગવડ કરી. કેદીઓની મુક્તિ માટેની ઝુંબેશમાં પણ જોરદાર કામ કર્યું.

આ સાથે દેશની આઝાદી માટેની લડત પણ પાછી ઉપાડી. બીજા આફ્રિકી અને કેન્યાવાસી એશિયનો સાથે મળી અનેક પત્રિકાઓ અને ભીંત પત્રો લખ્યા અને છપાવ્યા. ચોપાનિયાની વહેંચણી દેશભરમાં કરી અને ભીંતપત્રોને મધરાતે ગામના રસ્તે રસ્તે ચોંટાડ્યા.

૧૯૬૦માં ઓગીનૂગા ઓડીનૂગા તેમ જ જેમ્સ ગીચુરુ સાથે મળી પીટોએ એક કિસ્વાહીલી પખવાડિક ખબરપત્ર 'સાઉટી યા કાનુ' શરૂ કર્યું. આઝાદીની લડત જે આફ્રિકી જનતા અને નેતાઓ લડી રહ્યા હતા તેને એશિયન કેન્યાવાસીઓનો પૂરેપૂરો સાથ આપવા માટે ચનન સહિ, કે. પી. શાહ વગેરે સાથે મળી તેઓએ કેન્યા ફ્રિડમ પાર્ટીની સ્થાપના કરી.

આ વખત દરમ્યાન સામ્રાજ્યશાહીઓની કોશિશ હતી કે મજૂર સંઘના નેતાઓ ગદ્દારીના રસ્તા ઉપર ચડી જાય અને મજૂરોના હિત માટેની લડત છોડી દે. તેઓને એમ પણ જોઈતું હતું કે કેન્યાના સંઘો આફ્રિકી ખંડના બીજા સંઘો સાથે ભળીને સામ્રાજ્યશાહીને પડકાર ના કરે. બીજા મજૂરના નેતા જેવા કે ડેનીસ અક્રમુ સાથે મળી પીટોએ આનો સામનો કર્યો. એટલું જ નહિ પણ 'ઓલ આફ્રિકા ટ્રેડ યુનિયન ફેડરેશન' કે જેનું મથક ધાનામાં હતું તેની સાથે સંપર્ક

સાધ્યો અને આફ઼રિકી એકતા આગળ વધારી.

૧૯૬૧માં ઓગીનગ્ગા ઓડીનગ્ગા, જોસેફ઼ મુરુમ્બી અને પીટોએ પાન આફ઼રિકન પ્રેસની સ્થાપના કરી. પીટો તેના જનરલ મેનેજર બન્યા અને 'સાઉટી યા મ્વાફ઼કિા', 'પાન આફ઼રિકા' તેમજ 'ન્યાન્ઝા ટાઈમ્સ' નામના ત્રણ ખબરપત્રો છાપવાનું કામ શરૂ કર્યું.

પૂર્વ આફ઼રિકાની એકતા માટે તેમ જ કેન્યા, યુગાન્ડા અને ટાન્ગાનિકાનું એક સંઘ યાને ફેડરેશન બને તે માટે તેઓએ ઘણી કોશિશ કરેલ. ૧૯૬૩માં તેઓ ઈસ્ટ આફ઼રિકન સેન્ટ્રલ લેજસ્લિેટીવ એસેમ્બલીના સભ્ય તરીકે ચૂંટાયા.

૧૯૬૩ - આ જ વરસે તેઓ કેન્યાની રાજ્ય સભા, નેશનલ એસેમ્બલીના સભ્ય તરીકે પણ ચૂંટાયા, સભામાં જરા પણ પાછી પાની કર્યા વગર કામ કર્યું તે બદલ તેઓની 'બેક બેન્ચરસ ગ્રુપ'ના પબ્લસિીટી સેક્રેટરી તરીકની નમિણૂક તેઓના બીજા સાથીઓએ કરી.

૧૨ ડીસેમ્બર ૧૯૬૩ના રોજ કેન્યા આઝાદ થયું પરંતુ આફ઼રિકા ખંડમાં હજુ સામ્રાજ્યશાહીઓનો પગ હતો. મોઝામ્બીક, અંગોલા, રોડેશ્યા, દક્ષણિ આફ઼રિકા અને નામીબ્યાની આઝાદી માટે આ દેશોના દેશપ્રેમીઓ લડી રહ્યા હતા તેઓને પીટોએ ઉત્તેજન આપ્યું. પોર્ટુગીઝ સામ્રાજ્યશાહી જે લડાઈ મોઝામ્બીકમાં ચાલી રહી હતી તેને મદદ કરવા માટે મુઈનગ્ગા ચોક્વે સાથે મળી તેઓએ ૧૯૬૨માં મોમ્બાસામાં મોઝામ્બીક આફ઼રિકન નેશનલ યુનયિનની સ્થાપના કરવાની કોશિશ કરી, પરંતુ અંગ્રેજ સરકારે આ સંસ્થાને કોઈ પણ કામ કરવાની મનાઈ કરી. કેન્યાની આઝાદી પછી પીટોએ મોઝામ્બીકના સ્વતંત્રતાના લડવૈયા, ફ઼્રેલીમો સાથે સંપર્ક સાધ્યો. ઓર્ગેનાઈઝેશન ઓફ઼ આફ઼કિન યુનટિીની સ્વતંત્રતા સમતિમાં તેઓએ બીજા આફ઼રિકી મુલકોની આઝાદી માટે ઘણું કામ કર્યુ.

પીટોનું માનવું હતું કે દેશને રાજનીતિઆઝાદી મળે તે દેશની પ્રગતનિું પહેલું પગલું છે, ત્યારબાદ જનતાની આર્થકિ સ્થતિસિુધારવા માટે બીજા પણ પગલાં લેવા પડશે. દેશની તજિોરી ઉપરથી સામ્રાજ્યશાહીઓની બેંકો તેમ્ જ મોટી મોટી ઓદ્યોગકિ અને વેપારી કંપનીઓનો કબ્જો હઠાડવો પડશે. તે સાથે એવાં પણ પગલાં લેવાં જોઈએ કે જેથી દેશની મલિકત થોડાં જ માણસોના હાથમાં ન રહે પણ આખી જનતામાં તેની વહેંચણી થાય.

આવી માન્યતા રાખતા દેશપ્રેમીના દુશ્મનો ઘણા હોય તે સ્વભાવકિ છે. આવા કાયર દુશ્મનોએ આ શૂરવીર દેશપ્રેમી, પીઓ ગામા પીટોને ૨૪ ફ઼ેબ્રુઆરી ૧૯૬૫ના દિવસે ૩૮ વરસની ઉમરે ગોળીબાર કર્યા અને ત્યાં જ તેઓએ શહીદી વહોરી લીધી.

સૌજન્ય : "અલક મલક", ડિસેમ્બર ૧૯૮૫; પૃ. ૦૭-૦૯.

Pio Gama Pinto (1927-1965)

Pio Gama Pinto was born in Nairobi on 31 March 1927. His father sent him to India for education at an early age. On completing his education, he worked for some time in Post and Telecommunication Company in Mumbai. He participated in trade union activities and joined a strike to demand workers' rights.

Then he secretly entered Goa to work for the liberation of Goa from Portuguese imperialism. The imperialist government issued a warrant for his arrest but with the help of other freedom fighters he escaped from Goa and returned to Kenya in 1949.

Pinto worked as a clerk in Nairobi but when he saw the misery of the country under British imperialism he was inspired to join the freedom movement. In 1951, he started working at East African Indian Congress office which was housed in the Desai Memorial Building. He established contacts with the leaders and members of the African liberation movement, the Kenya African Union and trade unions and worked for the unity of Africans and Asians. In 1950 when the trade union leaders Chege Kibachia, Makhan Singh and Fred

Kubai were arrested, Pinto continued the union's activities along with the workers.

In order to work effectively, he learnt the Kiswahili language. He thought this was essential to be able to work closely with the African people.

To counter the propaganda of British imperialists he entered into the field of journalism. He became the editor of *Uzwod*, a newspaper in the Kokani language. He also published articles in the *Colonial Times*. In 1953, Pinto joined the Gujarati – English bilingual *Daily Chronicle* as an editor. He published a number of articles against the British Government with the help of D. K. Sharda, Haroon Ahmad and Pranlal Sheth.

On 20 October 1952, a fierce battle started between the freedom fighters and the imperialist army. Many African leaders and thousands of their followers were sent to prisons and detention camps. Land of many patriots was confiscated by the government. Innocent people were oppressed. Pinto and other patriots (such as Ambubhai Patel) exposed such dastardly acts of the government. Pinto also found lawyers for the freedom fighters who were being tried in court. Many Asian Kenyan patriots came forward to defend the freedom fighters against the government, fir example, F. R. De Souza, J. M. Nazareth, E. K. Nawroji, A. R. Kapila, S. M. Akram, A. H. Malik, Sheikh Amin, K. D. Trevadi, Arvind Jamindar.

Along with these activities, he also supplied arms and other materials to the Mau Mau fighters in conflict zones.

The British government was enraged by these activities. Pinto was arrested on 19 June 1954, and was sent to Takwa detention camp on Manda Island. His marriage to Emma had taken place just five months before his detention.

There were 200 other patriotic detainees at Manda including Achieng' Oneko, Muinga Chokwe and J. D. Kali. Pinto worked for the unity among them all. The government had conspired to create division among them through misinformation to make them give up their fight for freedom. To counter this, Pinto and others started word of mouth 'newsletters' to keep the morale high.

Pinto's father died while Pinto was in the detention camp. His father had requested the Government to let him see his son from his death bed. But the insensitive colonial Government, for whom he had faithfully worked for 30 years, flatly refused. The father died without seeing his son.

Pinto remained in Manda between 1954 and 1957 and in Kabernet between 1958 and 1959. After his release, he raised funds for the families of other detainees. He also campaigned for their release. For those of the detainees' family members having health problems, Pinto arranged free medical care from Asian Kenyan doctors such as Dr. Yusuf Eraj.

He continued his fight for freedom. Along with other Africans and Asian Kenyans, he printed and published leaflets which were then distributed all over the country. They also printed posters which they placed in public places at midnight.

In 1960, together with Oginga Odinga and James Gichuru, Pinto started a fortnightly newsletter in Kiswahili called *Sauti ya Kanu*. He also founded the Kenya Freedom Party along with Makhan Singh, K. P. Shah and others to provide the full support of Asian Kenyans to the African leaders and common people who were fighting for liberation.

During this period the imperialists attempted to lure the trade union leaders to betray the cause and give up their fight for workers' rights. They also wished that the Kenyan unions should not join hands with the other unions challenging imperialism in the rest of the African continent. Pinto fought against this along with other trade union leaders such as Dennis Akumu. More than this, he also established contacts with All Africa Trade Unions Federation whose headquarters were in Ghana, thus furthering the cause of African unity.

In 1961, Oginga Odinga, Joseph Murumbi and Pinto founded the Pan African

Press where they started publishing three newspapers: *Sauti ya Mwafrika, Pan Africa* and *Nyanza Times*. Pinto was the General Manager at the Press.

He worked hard for the unity of East Africa and the formation of a federation of Kenya, Uganda and Tanganyika. In 1963, he was elected a member of the East African Central Legislative Assembly.

In the same year he was elected to the National Assembly of Kenya too. He worked so fearlessly that the other members appointed him as the publicity secretary of the 'Back Benchers Group'.

On 12 December 1963, Kenya became a free nation. However, imperialism was still present elsewhere in the African continent. Pinto supported the freedom fighters in Mozambique, Angola, Rhodesia, South Africa and Namibia. To support the fight against Portuguese imperialism in Mozambique, he, with Muinga Chokwe, tried to form the Mozambique African National Union in Mombasa in 1962. But on getting wind of this endeavor, the British Government banned all their activities. After the liberation of Kenya, Pinto established contact with the freedom fighters of Mozambique. He contributed a great deal to the freedom of other African countries through the Freedom Committee of the Organisation of African Unity.

Pinto believed that political freedom was the first step to a country's progress. Other measures would be required to improve the economic condition of the people. The grip of imperialist banks and giant industrial and commercial firms would have to be removed. At the same time redistribution of wealth would be needed so that the wealth and resources of the country would not be concentrate in a few hands.

It is obvious that such a patriotic man would have many enemies among the vested interests. These dastardly people shot Pio Gama Pinto dead on 24 February 1965. Pinto was martyred at a young age of 38.

Alakmalak December 1985.

જસવંત સહિ ભારાજ (૧૯૩૫-); યાકુબદ્દીન; હસનુમનૂનાજી

૧૯૫૨માં શરૂ થયેલ કેન્યાની આઝાદીની સશસ્ત્ર લડતમાં જે ફાળો દેશપ્રેમી એશયિન કેન્યાવાસીઓએ કરેલ છે, તેનો ઇતિહાસ આજ સુધી ઘણો ખરો અનલખિતિ છે. ત્રીસ વરષનો ગાળો વીતી જવાથી આ અહેવાલ હવે તો ભૂલાવા પણ મંડાયો છે. આપણી ફરજ છે કે કોઈ પણ કસ્સિાઓ વિશે આપણી પાસે માહતિી હોય, તેને આપણે પ્રસદ્ધિ કરી, આપણા આ દેશમાંના ઇતહિાસની જાણ વધારીએ.

જશવંત સહિ ભારાજ વિશે આપણે વધારે જોઈએ તે પહેલાં એક-બે બીજા દેશપ્રેમીઓની જાણ કરીએ કે જેઓની જદિગી ઉપર વધારે પડતી માહતિી નથી, પરંતુ તેઓએ સ્વતંત્રતાની લડાઈમાં સહાયકારક કામ કર્યું હતું.

માઉ માઉની લડાઈ દરમ્યાન કરાટીના ગામની બાજુના ઈલાકામાં યાકુબદ્દીન નામના એક દેશપ્રેમી લાકડાની મીલ ચલાવતા હતા. ન્યાન્ડારુઆના જંગલમાં ઝાડ કાપવા જાય ત્યારે માઉ માઉના લડવૈયાઓ માટે અનાજ, કપડાં, જોડા, દવા અને બીજી અનેક જરૂરિયાતોની વસ્તુઓ તેઓ પહોંચાડતા. ઘણો વખત આ કામ કર્યા બાદ આ માહિતી અંગ્રેજ સામ્રાજ્યશાહીના જાસૂસને મળી અને ફિરંગી સરકારે તેઓને પકડવાનું કાવતરું કર્યું. પરંતુ આ સમાચાર સરકારમાં કામ કરતા કોઈ રાષ્ટ્રપ્રેમીએ યાકુબદ્દીનને પહોંચાડ્યા અને તેઓ વખતસર દેશની બહાર નીકળી ગયા. જો તેઓ પકડાયા હોત તો ફાંસીને માંચડે ચઢત. લડાઈના બાકીનાં વર્ષો તેઓએ પાકિસ્તાનમાં ગાળ્યા. કેન્યા સ્વતંત્ર થયા પછી તેઓ પાછા આવ્યા અને નાગરિકત્વ મેળવ્યું.

કરાટીનામાં જ હસનુમન્નાજી ટ્રાન્સપોર્ટરનું કામ ચલાવતા. આ સાથે લડાઈના આખા ગાળા દરમ્યાન તેઓએ લડવૈયાઓને અને તેઓના કુટુંબીઓ કે જેઓના વડીલો લડવામાં મશગૂલ હતા અથવા તો ફિરંગીઓના ડીટેન્સહન કેમ્પોમાં હતા તેઓને અનાજ અને બીજી ઘણી જરૂરિયાતો પૂરી પાડી. લડાઈને અંતે જ્યારે કાનુ પાર્ટીની પહેલી ચૂંટણી યોજાઈ, ત્યારે તેઓ આ ઈલાકાની શાખાના સભ્ય ચૂંટાયા હતા. લગભગ ૧૫ વરસ પહેલાં જ્યારે તેઓનું અવસાન થયું, ત્યારે તેઓની અંતિમ ક્રિયા માટે આખા પ્રાંતમાંથી ૨૦થી વધારે લોરીઓ ભરીને માણસો તેઓને છેલ્લે સલામ આપવા આવેલા.

નકુરુની નજીકના મોલો નામના ગામડામાં જસવંત સિંહ નામના એક કારીગર રહેતા હતા. તેઓ રિફ્ટ વેલી પ્રાંતમાં જે માઉ માઉના સિપાહી લડી રહ્યા હતા તેઓને છૂપી રીતે હથિયાર, કારતૂસ અને બંદૂકો બનાવવાની સામગ્રી પહોંચાડતા. આ આરોપસર તેઓને જુલાઈ ૧૯૫૪માં નકુરુની અદાલતમાં કાળી સજા કરવામાં આવેલ.

જસવંત સિંહ ભરાજનો જન્મ ૧૯૩૫માં લખપુર પંજાબમાં થયો હતો. તેઓના પિતા રેલવેમાં કામ મળવાથી ૧૯૧૪માં કેન્યા આવ્યા. ૫ વર્ષની ઉંમરે જસવંત કેન્યા આવ્યા. ૧૯૪૭માં તેઓ ભણતર માટે ભારત ગયા હતા. ત્યાં તેઓએ અંગ્રેજ સામ્રાજ્યશાહીની ગુલામી વિરુદ્ધી આંદોલનોનો ઊંડો અભ્યાસ કર્યો. તેઓ ભારતીય ઈન્કલાબી પક્ષ (રેવોલ્યુશનરી પાર્ટી ઑફ ઈન્ડિયા) કે જેનું માનવું હતું કે હથિયારબંધી લડત સિવાય ફિરંગીઓનો દેશ નિકાલ ના થઈ શકે – આ પક્ષના વિચારોની ભારે અસર થઈ.

જસવંત સિંહ ૧૯૫૩માં જ્યારે કેન્યા પાછા આવ્યા ત્યારે દેશમાં આઝાદીની લડત પૂર જોશમાં ચાલી રહી હતી. માઉ માઉના સ્વતંત્રતાના સૈનિકની વિરુદ્ધ લડવા માટે અંગ્રેજ શાસન

સત્તા અનેક જુવાનિયાઓને બળજબરીથી લશ્કર અને પોલીસ-ફોજમાં ભરતી કરતા. જસવંતને પરદેશી સરકારે કેન્યા પોલીસ રઝિર્વમાં દાખલ થવાની ફરજ પાડી. પરંતુ સામ્રાજ્યશાહી વિરુદ્ધ વિચારવાવાળા આ ક્રાંતિકારી યુવાનને એ ક્યાંથી પાલવે ! આ ઉપરાંત લશ્કરની કેળવણી દરમ્યાન ગોરા અફ્સરોના બીજી જાતના સિપાહીઓ પરત્યે અત્યાચારો પણ તેઓથી જોવાયા નહી.

જસવંત સહિ માઉ માઉના લડવૈયાઓ સાથે સંપર્ક સાધ્યો અને તેઓની સાથે મળી બંદૂકો બનાવવા માટે સાધન સામગ્રી એકઠી કરવાનું અને બંદૂકો અને બીજા હથિયારો બનાવવાનું કામ ઉપાડ્યું. મે ૧૯૫૪માં આવું કામ કરતાં તેઓ પકડાયા. તેઓની વિરુદ્ધ ફિરંગી અદાલતમાં મુકદમો ચાલ્યો અને ફાંસીને માંચડે ચડાવવાનો હુકમ બહાર પડ્યો. દેશપ્રેમી વકીલોની લડતોને લીધે મોતનો ચુકાદો જન્મકેદમાં બદલાયો. તેઓ માંડવા ટાપુમાં ટાકવા ડીટેન્શન કેમ્પમાં કેદ થયા. આ કેમ્પમાં સેંકડો કેદીઓમાં પીઓ ગામા પીન્ટોનો સમાવેશ હતો.

આ વર્ષો દરમ્યાન દેશમાં સશસ્ત્ર આઝાદીની લડાઈ સાથે રાજકીય આંદોલન પણ ચાલી રહ્યું હતું. રાષ્ટ્રપ્રેમીઓની એક માંગ હતી કે તમામ રાજકીય કેદીઓને સામ્રાજ્ય સરકારે કોઈ પણ શરત વિના છોડી મૂકવા જોઈએ. આ ઝુંબેશની સામે ફિરંગીઓ લાચાર બન્યા અને તેઓને કેદીઓને મુક્ત કરવાની ફરજ પડી. ૧૯૫૮માં જસવંત સહિની સાડાચાર વર્ષની કેદ ભોગવ્યા બાદ મુક્તિ થઈ.

લેખકની નોંધ :

આ લેખ અંબુભાઈ પટેલની ૧૯૮૬ઉમાં છપાયેલ ચોપડી 'સ્ટ્રગલ ફોર રીલઝિ જોમો કેન્યાટા એન્ડ હીઝ કલિગ્ઝ' પર આધારિત છે. કેદમાંથી નીકળ્યા બાદ જસવંત સહિ ભારાજ વશિ કોઈ વાચક પાસે માહિતી હોય તો લેખકને 'અલક મલક'ના સરનામે મોકલવા મહેરબાની કરશો. સૌજન્ય : "અલકમલક", ફેબ્રુઆરી ૧૯૮૬; પૃ. ૧૦-૧૧.

Jaswant Singh Bharaj (1935-); Yakub Deen and Hassan Manji

The contribution made by the patriotic Asian Kenyans to the fight for independence of Kenya has remained undocumented. After a lapse of thirty years, it is now being forgotten. It is our responsibility to record and bring to light any information we have regarding this phase of history.

Before we learn about Jaswant Singh Bharat in some detail, let us mention a couple of other patriots about whom we do not have much information, but who had also participated in the freedom struggle.

During the Mau Mau fight, a patriot named Yakub Deen was running a saw mill in the region next to Karatina village. When he went to Nyandarua forest to fell trees, he passed on grains, clothes, shoes, medicines and other provisions to the Mau Mau fighters. After some time, the secret intelligence agency of the imperialist government came to know about this and conspired to arrest him. But Yakub Deen was warned about this by a patriotic government employee and he immediately fled the country. Had he been arrested, he would have been hanged. While the war was going on, he remained in Pakistan. When Kenya won independence he returned and became its citizen.

Similarly, Hassan Manji was running a transport company in Karatina. He too supplied food and other necessary materials to the families of those who were engaged in fighting or who were in detention camps. At the end of the struggle, he was elected a member of this region's Kanu branch when the party held its first election. When he passed away 15 years ago, people came in lorry-loads from all over the province to pay their final homage to him.

In Molo village near Nakuru, there lived an artisan named **Jaswant Singh**. He secretly supplied materials to make arms, cartridges and guns to the Mau Mau fighters in Rift Valley province. He was sentenced in Nakuru court for this offence in 1954.

Jaswant Singh Bharaj was born in 1935 at Lakhpur in Punjab. His father had come to Kenya as a railway employee in 1914. Jaswant came to Kenya at the age of five. In 1947, he went to India for studies. He observed closely the Indian struggle against British imperialism. He was deeply influenced by the ideology of the Revolutionary Party of India which believed that the British could not be driven out of the country without an armed struggle.

When Jaswant Singh returned to Kenya in 1953, the fight for freedom was in full swing. The British rulers were forcing young people to join the police and army to buttress the fight against the Mau Mau freedom fighters. Jaswant was also forced to join the Kenya Police Reserve Squad. But how could an anti-imperialist revolutionary tolerate this? Moreover, he could not stand the torture of native policemen at the hands of white officers during training.

Jaswant Singh contacted the Mau Mau fighters and started collecting materials as well as making guns and other weapons. In May 1954, he was arrested for this offence. A trial was held in the British court and a death sentence was passed. But patriotic lawyers challenged it and it was reduced to life imprisonment. He was sent to Takwa detention camp on Manda Island. There were hundreds of prisoners, including Pio Gama Pinto, in this camp.

As this armed struggle for freedom was going on, a concurrent political struggle was also happening . The patriots demanded unconditional release of all political prisoners. The British were helpless against this demand and were compelled to release the prisoners. In 1958 Jaswant Singh was freed after having served four and half years in prison.

Author's Note: this article is based on "Struggle for Release of Jomo Kenyatta and his Colleagues" by Ambubhai Patel published by New Kenya Publishers in 1963. If readers have any information about Jaswant Singh after his release from prison, kindly pass it on to this writer. –Nazmi Durrani.

Alakmalak February 1986.

દેશપ્રેમી એશિયન કેન્યાવાસીઓની ઓળખાણ : પત્રકારો - સંપાદકો - પ્રકાશકો - મુદ્રકો(૧)

કેન્યાના અંગ્રેજ સામ્રાજ્યશાહી વિરોધી સંઘર્ષમાં અનેક દેશપ્રેમી એશિયન કેન્યાવાસી પત્રકારો, સંપાદકો, પ્રકાશકો, મુદ્રકો તેમ જ ચોપડી બાંધનારોએ ઘણો મોટો ફાળો આપેલો છે. આપણે પહેલાંના લેખોમાં મણિલાલ દેસાઈ, અંબુભાઈ પટેલ, પીઓ ગામા પીટો અને મખનસહિ વશિ જાણ કરી છે. આ સિવાય બીજા પણ ઘણા રષ્ટ્રભક્તોએ આ લડતમાં ભાગ લીધેલ, આ લડત હતી અંગ્રેજ શાસન સત્તાની જાતિય અને રંગ ભેદભાવની રાજ્યનીતિનિ પડકાર દેતી લડત અને દેશની આઝાદીની લડત.

આ દેશપ્રેમીઓના બાપદાદાઓ ભલે ભારત અથવા પાકિસ્તાનથી આવેલા, પરંતુ

67

તેઓની માન્યતા હતી કે એશયિન કેન્યાવાસીઓની વફાદારી કેન્યા પૂરત્યે પહેલી હોવી જોઈએ. આનો મતલબ એમ ન થયો કે આપણે આપણી અસલયિત ભૂલી જઈએ. આપણે આપણી સંસ્કૃતિ, આપણી ભાષાઓ વગેરેને ઉત્તેજન આપવું જોઈએ પણ એ સાથે આપણે એ પણ યાદ રાખવું જોઈએ કે જે દેશમાં આપણે જન્મ લઈએ એ દેશ આપણો, અહીની હવા અને અહીનાં અન્નપાણીથી આપણે પોષાયા, એટલે આ દેશ તરફની ભક્ત, એના તરફની વફાદારી એ આપણી ફરજ છે. આવી માન્યતા રાખવાવાળા આ દેશપ્રેમીઓ કેન્યાના ગોરા વિરોધી આંદોલનમાં પરોવાઈ ગયા. આ સાથે ભારતમાં જે સામ્રાજ્યશાહીની સામે સંઘર્ષ ચાલી રહ્યો હતો તેની સાથે પણ સંબંધ રાખ્યો. બન્ને દેશોની લડતના દુ:શ્મન એક હતા : અંગ્રેજ સામ્રાજ્યવાદ.

પત્રિકા કે ખબરપત્ર દ્વારા પરદેશી શાસન સત્તાને પડકાર કરવાવાળા સૌપ્રથમ કેન્યાવાસી એશયિન સીતારામ આચાર્ય હતા. તેઓ ૧૯૧૨માં દક્ષિણ ભારતથી પૂર્વ આફ્રિકા આવ્યા. અહી તેઓએ રેલવેમાં અને અંગ્રેજ લશ્કરમાં ટેલિગ્રાફરનું કામ કર્યું. ભારતમાં તેમ જ દુનિયાના બીજા મુલકોમાં વસેલા ભારતીયોએ ભેગા મળી સામ્રાજ્ય સરકારને પડકાર કરવા માટે એક છૂપો રાજકીય પક્ષ શરૂ કરેલ, આનું નામ હતું ગદ્દર પક્ષ. આ પક્ષની માન્યતા હતી કે બનિહથયિરી લડતથી પરદેશી કબજો આપણા દેશોમાંથી નહ નીકળે. આ કામ કરવા માટે સશસ્ત્ર બળવો પોકારવો પડશે.

ગદ્દર પક્ષની પૂર્વ આફ્રિકીના શાખાના નેતા આચાર્ય હતા. પહેલી વિશ્વ લડાઈ દરમ્યાન તેઓએ એક છૂપું ખબરપત્ર છપાવી અને તેની વહેંચણી કરી. આ વાતની જાણ ગોરાઓને થતા તેઓએ આચાર્યને દેશનિકાલ કર્યા અને પંજાબમાં તેઓને નજર કેદ રાખ્યા. જ્યારે ૧૯૧૫ની અંતમાં તેઓ પકડાયા ત્યારે અંગ્રેજોને બરાબર જાણ ન હતી કે આ પક્ષનું કામ અહી કેટલું બધું ફેલાઈ ગયું હતું. આ બાદ જે ગદ્દર પક્ષના સભ્યો પકડાયા તેઓને તો ફાંસી સુધીની સજા થયેલ. બે કેન્યાવાસી એશયિનો ૧૯૧૬માં ફાંસીને માંચડે ચઢ્યા અને બીજા તૂરણને બંદૂકથી મારી નાખવામાં આવેલ. આ સવાય આઠ માણસોને છ મહિનાથી લઈ ચૌદ વરસની જેલની સજા કરવામાં આવેલ અને એ ઉપરાંત વીસ માણસોને દેશમાંથી બળજબરીથી કાઢી મુકવામાં આવેલ. આ શૂરવીરો ઉપર આક્ષેપ મૂકવામાં આવેલ કે તેઓ પાસે ગુપ્ત પત્રિકાઓ મળેલ હતી કે જેમાં સામ્રાજ્ય વિરોધી માહતી હતી અને તેઓએ જનતાને અંગ્રેજો વિરૂદ્ધ ઉશ્કેર્યા હતાં.

વિશ્વ યુદ્ધ પૂરું થયા પછી સીતારામ આચાર્ય પાછા કેન્યા આવ્યા અને ૧૯૨૩માં તેઓએ મણિલાલ દેસાઈ અને એન. એસ. ઠાકુર સાથે મળી અંગ્રેજી ભાષામાં 'ડેમોક્રેટ' નામનું એક છાપું શરૂ કર્યું. આ છાપામાં તેઓએ સામ્રાજ્ય શાસન સત્તાની અન્યાય ભરેલી વર્તણૂકની

જાહેરાત આપી અને આફ્રિકી અને કેન્યાવાસી એશિયનોની લડતને જોરદાર ટેકો આપ્યો. દેશમાં વિલાયતી વસાહતોનાં છાપાઓમાં જે ખોટો પ્રચાર પ્રગટ થતો, તેની સામે તેઓએ 'ડેમોક્રેટ'માં ખરી હકીકત પ્રજા સામે રજૂ કરી. આ સિવાય તેઓએ પોતાના ખબરપત્રનું જે પ્રિન્ટિંગ પ્રેસ હતું તેમાં આફ્રિકી છાપાંઓ અને પત્રિકાઓ છાપવાનું કામ પણ કર્યુ. આ છાપાઓમાં કીકુયુ સેન્ટ્રલ એસોશિયેશનનું 'મ્વીગ્વીથાન્યા'નો સમાવેશ થાય છે. આના સંપાદક મૂઝે જોમો કેન્યાટા હતા.

ગિરધારીલાલ વદ્દિયાર્થી.

જેઓનું મૃત્યુ ૩૧ જુલાઈ ૧૯૮૫માં થયેલ, એ એક બીજા દેશપ્રેમી પ્રકાશક હતા. તેઓનો જન્મ ઓગષ્ટ ૧૯૦૩માં નાઈરોબીમાં થયો હતો. ૧૯૩૦માં તેઓએ હિંદી-ઉર્દૂ-અંગ્રેજી સાપ્તાહિક 'મતિરો' અને ૧૯૩૩માં ગુજરાતી-અંગ્રેજીમાં છપાતું 'કોલોન્યુલ ટાઈમ્સ' શરૂ કર્યાં. આ છાપું લગભગ ત્રીસ વરસ સુધી છપાયું. આ સિવાય આફ્રિકી જનતા સુધી સામ્રાજ્યશાહીઓના પ્રચાર વગરના સમાચાર પહોંચે તે માટે કસ્વિાહીલી ભાષામાં ૧૯૩૩માં 'હબારી ઝા દુનિયા' ('દુનિયાના સમાચાર') અને ૧૯૫૨માં 'જીચો' ('આંખ') નામના સાપ્તાહિક ખબરપત્રો પણ પ્રસિદ્ધ કરવાનું શરૂ કરેલ. આ બન્ને કસ્વિાહીલી છાપાંઓમાં જે ગોરાઓની ગેરવ્યાજબી રાજ્યનીતિ વિષે સમાચાર છપાતા તે પરદેશી શાસન સત્તાને પસંદ ના પડ્યું. તેથી તેઓએ 'હબારી'ને ૧૯૪૭માં અને 'જીચો'ને ૧૯૬૨માં બંધ કરવાની ફરજ પાડી.

પોતાના છાપાઓ પ્રસિદ્ધ કરવાની સાથે સાથે વદ્દિયાર્થીએ બીજા આફ્રિકી દેશપ્રેમીઓના ખબરપત્રો પણ છાપવામાં મદદ કરેલ. દાખલા તરીક એક નેતા જેમ્સ બ્યુટાહસે તેઓ વિષે નીચે મુજબ લખ્યું છે :
"૧૯૩૭માં મેં એક ખબરપત્ર પ્રસિદ્ધ કરવાનું શરૂ કર્યું કે જેનું નામ હતું 'મુથીથુ' ('ખજાનો') જો વદ્દિયાર્થીએ મને મદદ ન કરી હોત તો આ છાપું કદી પ્રગટ ન થાત. અમારી પાસે છપાવવા માટે પૈસા ન હતા. તેઓએ અમારા માટે બધું કમ્પોઝીંગનું તેમ જ છાપવાનું કામ કર્યુ. આમાં તેઓને ન કોઈ પૈસાની લાલચ હતી કે ન કોઈ અંગત સ્વાર્થ. તેઓને ફક્ત એમ જોઈતું હતું કે આફ્રિકીઓને પોતાના હકોની માંગ કરવાનો મોકો મળે."

આ સિવાય જુદા જુદા વખતે વદ્દિયાર્થીના કોલોન્યુલ પ્રિન્ટિંગ વર્ક્સે બીજા ઘણા ખબરપત્રો છાપ્યા. આમાં 'લુઓ મેગેઝીન' ૧૯૩૭માં અને ૧૯૪૦-૫૦ના દાયકા દરમ્યાન લુઓ ભાષામાં 'રામોગી' અને કીકુયુમાં 'મુમેન્યેયેરે'નો સમાવેશ છે.

સૌજન્ય : "અલક મલક", માર્ચ ૧૯૮૬; પૃ. ૬-૭.

Patriotic Kenyans:
Journalists, Editors, Publishers, Printers

(Part 1)

Many Asian Kenyans journalists, editors, publishers and book binders have contributed a great deal to the fight against British imperialism. We have discussed the role of Manilal Desai, Ambubhai Patel, Pio Gama Pinto and Makhan Singh. Apart from these, many other patriotic Asian Kenyans participated in the struggle. This fight was against the discriminatory policy of the British rulers and for the liberation of the country.

Though the forefathers of these patriots had migrated from India or Pakistan, they firmly believed that the first loyalty of Asian Kenyans must be to Kenya. This does not imply that we lose our identity. We must preserve our culture, our language but at the same time we must remember that the country where we are living is our home. We are nourished by this land. So we owe our loyalty, our dedication to this country. This spirit inspired the Asian Kenyans to join the fight for freedom. At the same time they also supported the Indian struggle against imperialism. They had a common enemy: British imperialism.

The first Asian Kenyans to challenge the foreign rule through print media was Sitaram Acharya. He had come from South India to East Africa in 1912. He worked in the railways and for the British army as a telegrapher. Some people in India and the Indians living abroad had founded a secret political party to challenge the imperialist government. This party was known as Ghadar Party. They believed in armed struggle against imperialism. They argued that armed revolt was needed to drive the foreign rulers out of the country.

Acharya was the leader of the East Africa Branch of Ghadar Party. During the First World War, he printed and distributed a secret newsletter. The British came to know about this. So Acharya was exiled and was kept under house arrest in Punjab. When he was arrested in 1915, the British rulers did not know to what extent the Ghadar Party had developed its activities. The party workers who were arrested after this were sentenced to death. Two Asian Kenyans were hanged and three others were shot dead in 1916. Eight persons were imprisoned for six months up to fourteen years. Twenty people were forcibly sent into exile. These brave men were accused of being in possession of seditious, anti-government leaflets and of inciting people against the British.

After the world war was over, Sitaram Acharya returned to Kenya. In 1923 he, together with Manilal Desai and N. S. Thukur, launched an English newspaper, *The Democrat.* Through this newspaper, he exposed the unjust policy of the imperialist rulers and vigorously supported the struggle of Africans and Asian Kenyans. He also countered the false propaganda carried out by the newspaper of the British settlers and, through *The Democrat*, presented a true picture to the public. In addition, he utilised his printing press to print African newspapers and pamphlets. This included Kikuyu Central Association's *Muigwithania,* whose editor was Jomo Kenyatta.

Yet another patriotic publisher was Girdharilal Vidyarthi who passed away on 31 July 1985. He was born in August 1907 in Nairobi. In 1930, he started the trilingual weekly magazine *Mitro* (Friends) in Hindi, Urdu and English. In 1933, he published the Gujarati–English newspaper, *Colonial Times*. He ran this newspaper for about thirty years. In order to provide true, accurate news to African people he started *Habari za Dunia* (News of the World) in Kiswahili language in 1933, and another weekly *Jicho* (The Eye) in 1952. The foreign rulers were not pleased with the criticism of their unjust policies published in these newspapers, so they banned *Habari* in 1947 and *Jicho* in 1962.

Apart from publishing his own newspapers, Vidyarthi helped in printing the newspapers of African patriots. For example, James Beauttah has acknowledged this in the following words: "In 1937, I started publishing a newspaper called *Muthithu* (Treasure). Without Vidyarthi's help. I could not have done this. We had no money to pay for printing. He did all the composing and printing for us. He did not have any financial gain or personal benefit. He only wanted an opportunity for Africans to demand their rights."

In addition, Vidyarthi's Colonial Printing Works printed many other newspapers. Among them were *Luo Magazine* in 1937, and during the 1940–50 decade *Ramogi* in the Dholuo language and *Mumenyereri* in Kikuyu.

Alakmalak March 1986.

પત્રકારો, સંપાદકો, પ્રકાશકો, મુદ્રકો – ભાગ ૨

એક બીજા કેન્યાવાસી એશિયન દેશપ્રેમી, હારુન અહમ્મદના સંપાદન નીચે 'કોલોન્યલ ટાઇમ્સે' એક જોરદાર પરદેશી હકૂમત વિરુદ્ધી ઝુંબેશ ઉપાડેલ. ઘણી શોષણખોરી અને જુલમી રાજ્યનીતિઓ સામે પડકાર કર્યો. દેશમાં જાતિ અને રંગભેદભાવની વર્તણૂક, આફ્રિકી ખેતીવાડીની જમીન બળજબરીથી ઝૂંટી લેવી, દેશની લેજસ્લેટીવ કાઉન્સિલમાં આફ્રિકી પ્રતિનિધિત્વ ન હોવાનું અને કેન્યાવાસી એશિયનોનું પ્રતિનિધિત્વ વલિયાતી વસાહતો કરતાં ઘણું ઓછું, મજૂરોની સંસ્થાઓને નાબૂદ કરવી અને તેઓના હકોની માંગને દબાવી દેવાની કોશિશ, આફ્રિકી મજૂરોને બળજબરીથી સરકારી નોંધણીપત્રકો ગળામાં તાંબાની ડબલી(કીપેડ)માં પહેરવા.

આવા અનેક સામ્રાજ્યશાહીઓના જુલમોના સમાચાર અને તેના વિરુદ્ધ અભિપ્રાય પ્રસિદ્ધ કરવાથી વલિયારથી તેમ જ તેઓના છાપાઓના પત્રકારો અને સંચાલકોને ગોરી સરકાર

તરફથી ઘણી તકલીફો ભોગવવી પડેલ. જ્યારે ૧૯૪૫માં બીજું વિશ્વ યુદ્ધ પૂરું થયું ત્યારે અંગ્રેજ સરકારે ગોરા સૈનિકોને કેન્યા આવવાનું ઉત્તેજન આપ્યું અને તેઓને દેશના ફળદ્રુપ પહાડી પ્રદેશમાં હજારો એકરો જમીન આપી. પરંતુ જ્યારે આફ્રિકી સૈનિકો અંગ્રેજ લશ્કરમાં બર્મા તેમ જ ઉત્તર આફ્રિકામાં લડાઈમાં ભાગ લઈ જ્યારે દેશ પાછા આવ્યા ત્યારે તેઓને કોઈ પણ જાતનો બદલો કે ઇનામ ના મળ્યો. આવા ભેદભાવની સામે જ્યારે 'કોલોન્યલ ટાઈમ્સે' વાંધો નોંધાવ્યો ત્યારે વટિયાર્થી ઉપર મુકદ્દમો ચલાવવામાં આવ્યો અને તેઓને ૨,૦૦૦ શલીંગનો દંડ ભરવો પડ્યો.

૧૯૪૬ માં નાઈરોબી ઇન્ડયિન નેશનલ કૉંગ્રેસના ભૂતપૂર્વ મંત્રી ડબલ્યુ. એલ. સોહનએ 'કોલોન્યલ ટાઈમ્સ'માં એક કાગળ લખેલ. આમાં તેઓએ અંગ્રેજ સામ્રાજ્યશાહી હકૂમત નીચેના મુલકોની રૈયત તરફ અંગ્રેજોની વર્તણૂકની સરખામણી જર્મનીના કોન્સનટ્રેશન કેમ્પોમાં કેદીઓ સાથેની વર્તણૂક સાથે કરેલ. આ અભિપ્રાયને ગોરી અદાલતે રાજદ્રોહી ઠરાવી સોહનને અને વટિયાર્થીને ચાર-ચાર મહિનાની સખત કેદની સજા કરેલ. આ સાથે 'કોલોન્યલ ટાઈમ્સ'ના એક સંચાલક, વનૂશીદારને એક મહિનાની સખત કેદની સજા ભોગવવી પડેલ.

સોહને અદાલતમાં જે ન્યાય કરવાનો ઢોંગ થઈ રહ્યો હતો તેને પડકારતા કહ્યું : "હું માનું છું કે હું અંગ્રેજોનો ગુલામ છું. મારું એમ પણ માનવું છે કે દરેક ગુલામની પવિત્ર ફરજ છે કે તે પોતાની ગુલામીની હાલત સામે બળવો પુકારે. ગુલામ તરીકેની મારી ફરજ એમ પણ છે કે હું સર્વ ગુલામો પાસે બળવાનો સંદેશો પહોંચાડું. આમાં જ પીડાતી અને ગુલામી ભોગવતી માનવતાનો છુટકારો છે."

જેલની બહાર નીકળ્યા પછી પણ સોહનએ સામ્રાજ્યશાહીઓની સામે ટક્કર લેવાનું ના મૂક્યું. આથી એક વખત જ્યારે તેઓ ભારત કોઈ કામ અર્થે ગયા અને જ્યારે પાછા આવવાનો પ્રયત્ન કર્યો, તો શાસન સત્તાએ તેઓને દેશમાં દાખલ થવાની મનાઈ કરી દીધી. અંગ્રેજ સરકારને સોહનથી ડરવાનું બીજુ કારણ એ હતું કે તેઓની કોશિશ હતી કે સામ્રાજ્ય વિરુદ્ધી ઝુંબેશમાં આફ્રિકિઓ અને કેન્યાવાસી એશિયનો હાથ મળાવીને કામ કરે. દાખલા તરીકે તેઓની આ કોશિશને કારણે નવેમ્બર ૧૯૪૪માં જે ઇસ્ટ આફ્રિકિન નેશનલ કૉંગ્રેસની સભા ભરાયેલ તેમાં કેન્યા આફ્રિકિન સ્ટડી યુનયિનના પ્રમુખ જેમ્સ ગીચુરુ હાજર રહેલ. આની સામે અંગ્રેજ પદ્ધતિહતી માણસને માણસથી અલગ કરીને શાસન કરવાની.

સૌજન્ય : "અલક મલક", અપ્રિલ ૧૯૮૬; પૃ. ૬-૭.

74

Patriotic Kenyans:
Journalists, Editors, Publishers, Printers (Part 2)

Haroon Ahmed, another Asian Kenyans patriot, was the editor of *Colonial Times* which vigorously opposed foreign rule and challenged exploitation and oppression. He raised his voice against racial discrimination against the forceful confiscation of African land, the lack of African representation in the Legislative Council, and the under–representation of Asian Kenyans as compared to the British settlers. He was also vocal against the destruction of workers' unions, the suppression of their demands for rights and the compulsory registration of workers who were then forced to display identification tags hanging around the neck in a copper box (Kipande).

Vidyarthi and his fellow journalists exposed these unjust policies and expressed opinions against them. This invited the wrath of the imperialist rulers who harassed them in many ways. In 1945 when the Second World War ended, the British government encouraged white soldiers to settle in Kenya and gave them thousands of acres of fertile land in the Highlands. On the other hand, when the African soldiers fighting for the British Army in Burma and North Africa returned to their country, no reward or bonus was given to them. When the *Colonial Times* opposed this discrimination, Girdharilal Vidyarthi was tried in court and fined 2,000 shillings.

In 1946, the former secretary of Nairobi Indian Congress, W. L. Sohan wrote a letter in *Colonia Times*. In this letter, he compared the treatment of the subjects under the British imperialist rule to the plight of the prisoners in German concentration camps. The British court branded this opinion as sedition and both Sohan and Vidyarthi were sent to prison for four months. Along with them, another *Colonial Times* journalist, Vanshidar, was imprisoned for a month.

Challenging the farce of the trial in the court, W. L. Sohan said:

> I believe that I am a slave of the British. I also believe that it is the pious duty of every slave to revolt against his slaver. As a slave, it is also my duty to take the message of revolt to all other slaves. This is the only way to liberate the victims of suffering and slavery.

Even after being released from prison, Sohan continued his fight against the imperialists. So when he travelled to India on a business, he was not allowed to enter the country on his return. Another reason why the British Government was afraid of Sohan was his mission to unite African and Asian Kenyans in their fight against imperialism. By its very nature, the British policy of divide and rule stood strongly against this. For example, as a result of his efforts, the president of Kenya African Study Union, James Gichuru, attended the Conference of East African National Congress held in November 1944.

Alakmalak April, 1986.

૧૯૪૭માં ગુજરાતી-અંગ્રેજી ભાષાઓમાં છપાતું એક બીજું ખબરપત્ર 'ડેઇલી ક્રોનકિલ' શરૂ થયું. આના સંસ્થાપકો હારુન આહમદ, પીઓ ગામા પીટો, પ્રાણલાલ શેઠ, ડી. કે. શારદા, મખનસહિ, ચનન સહિ અને લેજીસ્લેટીવ કાઉન્સલિના સભ્ય એ. બી. પટેલ હતા. મણિલાલ દેસાઇનું 'ઇસ્ટ આફ્રિકન ક્રોનકિલ' તેમ જ સીતારામ આચાર્યનું 'ડેમોક્રેટ'નો જે સામ્રાજ્યશાહી વિરુદ્ધી પદ્ધતનો દાખલો હતો તે 'ડેઇલી ક્રોનકિલે' અનુસર્યો. આ છાપાના સંપાદકો હારુન આહમદ અને પીટો હતા.

માઉ માઉનો સ્વતંત્રતાની લડાઇ વિષે તપાસ કરવા માટે અંગ્રેજ સરકારે ફોરફ્લિડ નામના એક ગોરાની નિમણુક કરેલ. ફોરફ્લિડે પોતાના વર્તમાન પત્રમાં 'ડેઇલી ક્રોનકિલ' વિષે લખેલ કે આ છાપાએ દેશની આફ્રિકી જનતાના હકોની માંગની લડતને જરા પણ પાછી પાની

કર્યા વગર ટેકો આપેલ. અંગ્રેજ ગવર્નર ફ઼િલીપ મીચલને આ ખબરપત્રના કર્મચારીઓની જે કેન્યા પૂરત્યે દેશપ્રેમની વર્તણૂક હતી, તેને અંગ્રેજ સામ્રાજ્ય સામે રાજદ્રોહી જેવી લાગી.

૧૯૪૭થી ૧૯૫૦ના ગાળા દરમ્યાન આ છાપા ઉપર પચાસથી વધારે વખત રાજદ્રોહના આરોપ સબબ મુકદ્દમા કરવામાં આવેલ. ૧૯૪૭માં મોમ્બાસાના મજૂરોએ પોતાના હકોની માંગ કરતાં એક સાર્વત્રકિ હડતાલ બોલાવેલ. 'ફ઼્રોનક઼િલ' આ હડતાલને પૂરેપૂરો ટેકો આપ્યો. આ સાથે અંગ્રેજ સરકારે મજૂરો તેમ જ તેઓના નેતાઓ સામે જે સખત ગેરવ્યાજબી પગલાં લીઘેલ તેની સામે પડકાર કર્યો. આ કારણસર તૂયારના સંપાદક હારુન આહમદને છ મહિનાની કેદ ભોગવવી પડેલ.

આ દેશપ્રેમીએ 'કોલોન્યલ ટાઈમ્સ' અને 'ડેઈલી ફ઼્રોનક઼િલ'માં એક પત્રકાર તરીકે જે લડત લડ્યા તે સવિાય રાજકીય સંઘર્ષ તેઓએ બીજા ક્ષેત્રમાં પણ ચાલુ રાખી. દાખલા તરીકે ઓક્ટોબર ૧૯૪૬માં તેઓએ ભારતીય યુવાન સંઘ(ઇન્ડયિન યુથ લીગ)ના આશ્રય હેઠળ એક ગંજાવર મોર્ચો યોજ્યો કે જેમાં દક્ષણિ આફ્રિકાના નાગરકિોની લડતને ટેકો આપવામાં આવેલ. મોર્ચા પછી જે સભા બોલાવવામાં આવેલ તેમાં અનેક નેતાઓ એ ભાષાણો કર્યાં તેમાં જોમો કેન્યાટા અને આહમદનો સમાવેશ હતો. આહમદની કોશશિ હતી કે અંગ્રેજ સામ્રાજ્યશાહી સામેની લડતમાં કેન્યાના આફ્રિકી અને એશયિાઈ લોકો સાથે મળી કામ કરે.

૧૯૫૩માં આહમદ હીરાભાઈ પટેલ નામના એક વકીલે સાથે મળી ગુજરાતી ભાષામાં 'આફ્રિકા સમાચાર' નામનું સાપ્તાહકિ શરૂ કરેલ. આમાં પણ તેઓએ સર્વ નાગરકિોના હકોની બરાબરી અને લોકશાહીની જોરદાર માંગ કરવાનું ચાલુ રાખ્યું. એશયિન કેન્યનો વચ્ચે જે હદ્દિ-મુસલમાનના ભેદભાવો ઊભા થયેલ તેને હટાવવાનો તેઓએ પ્રયત્ન કર્યો. આ સાથે દેશની આફ્રિકી અને એશયિાઈ જનતા વચ્ચેનું જુદાપણું પણ દૂર કરવાની તેઓની કોશશિ ચાલુ રહી.

આવા પત્રકારો સવિાય બીજા દેશપ્રેમી પ્રકાશકો અને મુદ્રકો પણ હતાં કે જેઓએ સામ્રાજ્યશાહીઓ સામેની લડતમાં પોતાના અંગત સ્વાર્થનો જરા પણ વચિાર ના કર્યો. દાખલા તરીકે વી. જે. પટેલ નામના એક પ્રકાશકે હેનરી મુઓર્યાના કીકુયુ ભાષાનું ખબરપત્ર 'મુમેન્યેરેરે' છાપવાના આક્ષેપ ઉપર જેલમાં ગયેલ. આ પછી જૂન ૧૯૫૦માં તેઓ તેમ જ શ્રીમતી બેસન્ત કૌર, અમરસહિ અને તેમલ સહિને એક મહિનાની કેદ થયેલ. આ વખતે તેઓ એક બીજા દેશપ્રેમી ખબરપત્રમાં અંગ્રેજ સરકાર વશિોઘી લખાણ છાપવાનો આક્ષેપ હતો. આ છાપું હતું કે. સી. કમાઉ અને વક્ટિર મુરાગેનું 'હીડીયા ગીકુ યુ.'

એક બીજા દેશપ્રેમી પત્રકાર હતા ડી. કે. શારદા કે જેઓએ ૧૯૪૭-૫૧ દરમ્યાન 'ઉઈલી ક્રોનકિલ'માં કામ કરેલ. ત્યાર બાદ તેઓએ પોતાનું સાપ્તાહિક, 'ટ્રીબ્યુન' પ્રસિદ્ધ કરવાનું શરૂ કર્યું. આ છાપામાં તેઓ રંગ અને જાતિય ભેદભાવ દૂર કરવાની જોરદાર માંગ કરેલ. તેઓની એમ પણ કોશિશ હતી કે એશિયન કેન્યનોની બરાદરીના લોકોમાં જે હિંદુ, મુસલમાન અને ક્રિશ્ચિયન ધર્મોના ફાંટા પડેલ હતા, તે હટાડી દેવામાં આવે. તેઓને એમ પણ જોઈતું હતું કે સામ્રાજ્ય સરકાર સામેની લડતમાં આફ્રિકી અને એશિયાઈ લોકો સાથે મળી અને રાજકીય પક્ષોની સ્થાપના કરે. આવી બધી એકતાની કોશિશોએ અંગ્રેજ શાસન સત્તાને ગભરાવી મૂકી એટલે ૧૯૫૨ના અંતમાં માઉ માઉના કટોકટીના કાયદાઓ હેઠળ 'ટ્રીબ્યુન'નો અટકાવ કરવામાં આવ્યો.

આ બધા એશિયન કેન્યન દેશપ્રેમીઓ કે જેઓએ આપણા દેશની આઝાદીની લડતમાં પૂરેપૂરો અને નિસ્વાર્થ ભાગ લીધેલો તેઓ આપણા માટે ગર્વ પાત્ર છે. દેશ પરત્વેની લાગણી અને વફાદારીનો જે દાખલો તેઓ આપણા માટે રાખી ગયા છે તેનું પાલન કરવું એ આપણી ફરજ છે

જય કેન્યા

સૌજન્ય : "અલક મલક", મે ૧૯૮૬; પૃ. ૬-૭.

Patriotic Kenyans:

Journalists, Editors, Publishers, Printers (Part 3)

I n 1947 yet another bilingual Gujarati–English newspaper, *The Daily Chronicle*, was published. It founders were Haroon Ahmed, Pio Gama Pinto, Pranlal Sheth, D. K. Sharda, Makhan Singh, Chanan Singh and Legislative Council Member A. B. Patel. *The Daily Chronicle* followed the anti-imperialist policy of Manilal Desai's *East African Chronicle* and Sitaram Acharya's *The Democrat*. Haroon Ahmed and Pinto were its editors.

The British Government had appointed a Briton called Corefield to investigate the Mau Mau freedom fight. Corefield wrote in his report that the *Daily Chronicle* newspaper strongly supported the fight for African people's rights through its aggressively anti-imperialist editorial policy. The British Governor Philip Mitchell regarded this patriotic attitude towards Kenya as sedition and against the British Empire.

Between 1947 and 1950, over fifty sedition cases were filed against this newspaper and trials were held. In 1947, the workers in Mombasa went on a general strike to demand their rights. The *Daily Chronicle* fully supported this strike. It challenged the severe, unjust steps taken by the British Government against the striking workers and their leaders. For this, the then Editor Haroon Ahmed was sent to prison for six months.

Apart from his fight as a journalist through *Colonial Times* and *Daily Chronicle,* patriot man [Haroon Ahmed] carried on the political struggle in other fields as well. For example, in October 1946 under the auspices of the Indian Youth League, he organised a protest march in support of South Africa's freedom struggle. The march turned into a general meeting which was addressed by prominent leaders. Among them were Jomo Kenyatta and Ahmed. Ahmed went to great lengths to bring African Kenyans and Asians together in their fight against British imperialism.

In 1953, together with the lawyer Hirabhai Patel, Ahmed started a Gujarati weekly *Africa Samachar*. Through this magazine also he continued to demand equal rights for all and a democratic rule. He also tried to remove the division between Hindus and Muslims among Asian Kenyans. At the same time, he endeavoured to unite African and Asian people in Kenya.

Apart from these journalists, there were other patriotic publishers and printers too. They supported the fight against imperialism without any selfish motive. For example, publisher V. J. Patel was sent to prison for printing Henry Muoria's Kikuyu language newspaper *Mumenyereri*. Again in June 1950, he was imprisoned for a month along with Mrs. Besant Kaur, Amar Singh and Temal Singh. This time they were accused of printing an anti-government article in another nationalistic newspaper. This newspaper was *Hindi ya Gikuyu* published by K. C. Kamau and Victor Murage.

Another patriotic journalist was D. K. Sharda. He worked at *Daily Chronicle* during 1947–51. Thereafter he started publishing his own weekly newspaper *Tribune*. He demanded the abolition of discrimination on grounds of colour and race. He also endeavoured to remove the Hindu–Muslim–Christian divisions among Asian Kenyans. He wanted the African and Asian people to unite and form a political party to fight against imperialism. These efforts to bring about unity made the British rulers nervous. So towards the end of 1952, they banned the publication of *Tribune* under the Mau Mau Emergency Act.

We are indeed proud of these Asian Kenyans patriots who vigorously and selflessly participated in the fight for freedom. It is our duty to follow their example of patriotism and loyalty.

Alakmalak May 1986.

Film Review:
Moolu Manek (Gujarati, 1977)

ઐતિહાસિક અવલોકન ભારતીય ચલચિત્રો દ્વારા

મૂળુ માણેક :

The film, *Moolu Manek* was produced in 1977 by Shantilal Shah, directed by

Munilal Vyas, and the music was by Gaurang Vyas. This S. K. Films' movie had Shrikant Soni and Sarla Thevlekar in lead roles.

The historical event shown in 'Moolu Manek' took place at the beginning of the 19th century in Okha-Dwarka district of North Kathiawad. The Wagher people of this region had defended their freedom from the British East India Company whose rule was known as Company Government. The symbols of their freedom were swords and guns.

In this movie, the leaders of these martial and patriotic people are Moolu Manek and his uncle Jodha Manek. The film starts with a scene showing the preparations of Moolu's wedding to Shyambai. Right at this moment, the Company Government sends order for Waghers to surrender their arms to the British. The Waghers know that without the arms they would lose their freedom. So they refuse to give up their arms and declare an open revolt against the foreign aggressors. They also decide to fight against the native landlords who are traitors. One of these traitors is the ruler of Dwarka who collaborates with the British to oppress the people. He kidnaps women and rapes them. One such woman challenges Moolu and his companions to fight against the oppressor and kills herself. The Waghers vow by her blood that they would either free the country or give their lives fighting for freedom. But this causes dissidence between Moolu and his close friend Devu. Apart from being a friend, Devu is Moolu's would be brother-in-law as he is engaged to Moolu's sister. Moreover, Devu is in service of the Company Government as a colonel of a regiment. To protect his job Devu betrays his people and country. He loses Moolu's friendship and his fiancée breaks their engagement. When there is a conflict between personal love and love for the country this brave girl leaves her traitor lover and joins the fight for freedom.

Waghers make preparations for the fight, attack Dwarka and get victory. The fight continues and all patriotic fighters – men, women, elders, children, farmers, traders, poets and everyone else join in. People are inspired through folk songs, dances and devotional songs (Bhajans). Everyone takes up arms –

lathi (sticks), sword, gun, dragger – whatever is handy. Those who are unable to fight collect provisions for the fighters. Others collect secret information regarding the movement of the British army.

This fight for freedom disrupts social life. Moolu sends a message to Shyambai that their marriage cannot take place. The war is not likely to end in the near future, so she is free to marry someone else. But Shyambai is also a patriotic woman. She is proud of Moolu for whom the motherland is more important than personal happiness. She takes a vow to wait for Moolu against her father's wish. She starts supporting the fighters. Her father prevents her from supplying food to the fighters and pressures her to get married to someone else. But with the help of her mother she runs away from home and joins the fighters.

On the one hand we see the dignified conduct of these patriots and, on the other, we see the shameless and wicked behaviour of the British and the traitors. The British Chief General Herbert and his Indian stooges are busy enjoying *mujara* dance and molesting women.

The war goes on and the nationalist fighters win victories in many battles. They liberate many regions which were ruled by the British and their stooges. When the British army fails to defeat the patriots, General Herbert and Devu hatch a dastardly conspiracy. They believe that if Moolu is captured the fight will end. They do not realise that if one Moolu is dead, many others will take his place.

They capture Shyambai through deception. They then send a message to Moolu that if he wants Shyambai to be freed, he should surrender himself to the British. Moolu and Jodha disguise themselves as Sanyasi (Hindu hermit) and enter Devu's house where Shyambai is confined. They tie up Devu and free Shyambai with his mother's help. But Jodha Manek is captured by Devu. Devu is planning to chop off his head, hang it outside the village and challenge Moolu to recover it.

During the war, Devu's patriotic mother tries hard to convert Devu into a patriot. But Devu is intoxicated with the wealth and power given to him by the British. When Devu's mother becomes aware of Devu's plan, she tries to persuade him to give it up. But Devu refuses to do so. At last this patriotic woman decides to sacrifice her own life. She lies down in place of Jodha Manek's dead body. Unknowingly Devu cuts off his mother's head. But on seeing his mother's blood on his hands, he wakes up, and comes to his senses.

Part 2

The war continues and slowly the British aggressors get an upper hand. They succeed in breaking the contact between the fighters and the people. The fighters cease to get supplies of food and other materials. They and their children are starving. Moolu is upset to see their misery. He asks them to give up their arms for the sake of their children. But they refuse.

At this juncture, Devu who has now turned a patriot, appears. He apologises and asks the fighters not to give up their arms. He warns that if they surrender, the British will not show any mercy. They have no choice but to fight on to break the chains of slavery. Listening to Devu's words, the fighters vow again to overthrow the British rule.

They know that they will be vanquished in this way. But they are not afraid. They believe that their sacrifice will inspire other fighters, and this war will continue until the liberation of the country. Thus they get ready for the final battle, sacrifice their lives and set a shining example for the future freedom fighters.

The music of 'Moolu Manek' is melodious. The words of the songs are meaningful. The song sung by the bard, *The Waghers hit back with sticks* and Devu's last song *Do not give up arms* are very effective. The dances are appropriate. Before the fight begins people play Ras-Garba with sticks and at the time of victory they dance with swords and guns instead of sticks.

Another interesting part of the film is the role of a woman in the society. On the one hand, women are shown in the traditional roles of mother, sister and wife. On the other hand, their role changes as the fighting progresses. Women fully participate in the war. For example, Monghi and other women collect food and information for the fighters. Devu's mother brings her son to the right path by sacrificing her life. Shyambai, Moolu's sister and others take up arms and unite the army. Even when Moolu gets disheartened, these women remain firm.

Traditionally, women are taught to obey their fathers and husbands. But what if the man becomes a traitor? The answer is in the way Shyambai and her mother act. Shyambai joins the army against her father's wish, and her mother helps her defy her husband. Moolu's sister leaves her fiancé Devu who is in league with the enemy. Thus the film brings out the courageous and patriotic spirit of Indian women.

This marvellous film is available on video as well.

Alakmalak Diwali issue. October-November 1986

Remembering Heroes and their Achievements

The Revolutionary who supplied Arms and Ammunition to the Bush Fighters.

Mr. JASWANT SINGH BHARAJ

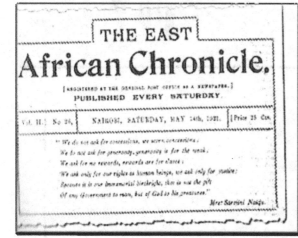

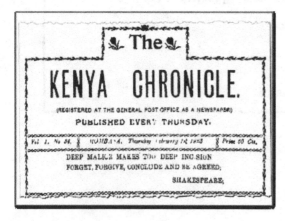

Figure 19: Kirtiyan di kaamyaabi (1937)

SOURCE: Makhan Singh Archives digitation project:

Nairobi Workers Strike
OUR DEMANDS.

For the information of the general public and those concerned this is to notify that the demands of the workers who are on strike at various works are the following:

1 Eight hours day.
2 25 percent increase in wages.
3 Recognisation of the Labour Trade Union of East Africa.
4 Taking back those workers who have struck.

Up till now the following employers have granted to their employers the above demands:

1 Tafail Mohamed, Contractor.
2 S. Nanak Singh, Furniture Maker.
3 Jogat Singh Bains, Contractor.
4 Karam Ali Nathoo, Box Body Maker.
5 Messrs. Thaker Singh & Co.,
6 Karam Chand, Furniture Maker.
7 N. B. Shah, Furniture Maker.

Makhan Singh,
Hon. Secretary,
Nairobi, 5.4.37.   The Labour Trade Union of E. A

A revolutionary
Kenyan Trade Unionist

Edited by Shiraz Durrani

LTUEA HANDBILL, 1935 (KHALSA PRESS)

A workers' mass meeting will be held on Saturday, 16th January, at 5.00 p.m. in the Ramgharia Plot (Campos Ribero St.) to decide effective methods to achieve the demands of Railway artisans and the demand of 25% increase in wages from 1st April. Please do attend. Long Live Workers' Unity - Makhan Singh, Sec. Labour Trade Unions

First annual conference of LTU Leaflet)1937

THE OPEN SESSION

of the

First Annual Conference

of

THE LABOUR TRADE UNION

OF EAST AFRICA

will be held on

Sunday, the 18th July, 1937,

From 9 a.m. to 1 p.m.

in the

Theatre Royal.

A concrete programme to improve the condition of workers of East Africa will be decided upon, the report of activities and accounts of the Labour Trade Union will be presented, lectures by prominent speakers will be delivered, and important resolutions will be moved.

All the workers, sympathisers and members of the Union are requested to attend.

MAKHAN SINGH,
Secretary,
Labour Trade Union E.A. Nairobi.

Khoja Press, Nairobi

Figure 20: First annual conference of LTU (1937)

Kenyatta-Makhan Singh-Odinga.

Kenyatta with Makhan Singh and Satwant Kaur.

From 1ˢᵗ November 1936, the Union began publishing a monthly paper called Kenya Worker. Three issues were published in Punjabi and one in Urdu. The Union's plans were to publish the paper also in English, Gujarati and Swahili. Makhan Singh was its editor. A few months later the paper was named East African Kirti. Its Editor was Mota Singh, the President of the Union at that time. The paper stopped after three issues had been published. This was due to the Government having prosecuted the editor for not having obtained registration for the paper. He was fined for the "offence". Both the papers contained articles about the Union's policies and news about workers' struggles and national and international news of general interest.*

The Annual Return made under the Newspaper Registration Ordinance indicated that East African Kirti was published weekly and that the average circulation was 1,000 copies per week.

Source: Durrani, Shiraz (2006): Never Be Silent: Publishing and Imperialism in Kenya, 1884 1963. pp.252-262. London, Nairobi: Vita Books. Available from African Books Collective. orders@africanbookscollective.com.

South Asian Kenyan Resistance in Historical Context

Durrani, Naila (1987): South Asian Kenyan Participation in People's Resistance

Durrani, Naila (1987): A brief outline of South Asian Kenyan participation in people's resistance against imperialism, 1884-1963.

Paper presented at the launch of the United Movement for Democracy in Kenya (Umoja). London, 1987.[7]

Introduction

The Berlin Conference of 1884 is a landmark in the history of the third world. It sanctioned the arbitrary partition of Africa, with each of the western powers carving out for itself as much of the continent as possible.

The advent of British colonialism in Kenya with its attendant economic structures of imperialism and class exploitation, led to a rapid transformation of Kenyan society to capitalism.

---

7. This article was prepared for presentation to the Umoja Conference (1987) and was not meant to be an academic paper, quoting sources etc. However, appropriate sources were used in compiling it. It is only being included in this publication as a historic record to serve as a brief reminder to all Kenyans and in particular South Asian Kenyans of their role in Kenya's history which does not get mentioned very often and lies buried. Apologies are offered to any Asian Kenyan participants in the struggle as well as to their families and friends if their names have been left out here and deserved to be mentioned.

Material in this article was used in the book by Durrani, S (2006): Never be Silent, Publishing and Imperialism in Kenya, 1884-1963. London: Vita Books.

By 1920, Kenya had been forced to the status of a colony, subjugated to unprecedented economic and political oppression of peasants and workers. Such a humiliating enslavement led to intensified Kenya people's resistance and eventually to political independence of Kenya in 1963.

However, as has happened in other countries, political independence did not lead to the complete overhaul of the imperialist economic structures. Nonetheless, it was a significant victory for the Kenyan people.

The actual process of imperialism in various countries had set into motion a chain of events with worldwide reverberations. Hence the landmarks in Kenya's history of resistance against imperialism should not be seen in isolation but in an international context.

Historically, these landmark events of the period 1884-1963 can be grouped into three sub-sections: 1884-1920; 1920-1945; and 1945-1963.

The waves of events which unfolded in each of these periods build up to a historical pattern. To simplify, these can be identified as the intrusion of imperialism; its capitalist form of exploitation of peasants and workers; contradictions that arose between the exploiter and the exploited; the struggles that ensued in response to colonial repression; and the resulting victories.

Each wave, however, had its own particularity. Thus, between 1884-1920, on the international scene, imperialist rivalry intensified and led to the First World War. It also saw the birth of the Socialist Revolution of 1917 in the Soviet Union.

Its reverberations were taken up in Kenya as the workers began to organise themselves through the trade union movement and political activism against the colonialists. Their activities reached a landmark with Harry Thuku the trade union leader's arrest and detention by the colonial authorities in 1922, the protest demonstration against his arrest led by Mary Muthoni Nyanjiru, and the subsequent massacre of workers by the colonial police and by the settlers at the nearby Norfolk Hotel.

The second wave, 1920-1945, encompassed the further sharpening of imperialist rivalries leading to the Second World War with the rise of fascism under Hitler and Mussolini.

In Kenya, this period recorded an increase in exploitation and sharpening of contradictions. The ensuing struggle against imperialism led to the consolidation of the trade union movement, independent education, and the ultimate rejection by the Kenyan masses of the Kikuyu Central Association (KCA) and Kenya African Union (KAU) policies of petition and constitutional methods of struggle which did not offer the economic and political freedom that people wanted.

The third wave, 1945-1963, came to a head with the political independence of India in 1947 and the people's revolution and victory in China in 1949. This led to new and revolutionary ideas in Kenya as well as everywhere else in the world.

At the same time, rebellion in Kenya became more militant and brought about the armed struggle of the Kenya Land and Freedom Army (KLFA or "Mau Mau," the name by which it came to be more commonly known). One of the generals in the KLFA was even named General "China" in glorification of people's victories in China. Finally, the armed struggle hastened the dawn of political independence in Kenya in 1963.

South Asian Kenya Participation
It is against this backdrop of links between the international and national events that the Asian Kenyans' resistance, as that of the other Kenyan nationalities, needs to be analysed. Initially, the Kenya people's resistance to their fertile

lands being taken away by the foreigners was based on nationality lines among the peasants. Later, as a working class emerged in urban and rural areas in response to the building of the railway and setting up of railway maintenance and other industries, class formation and class alliances of workers and peasants took shape, cutting across nationality, race and sex boundaries.

Over a period of about a thousand years prior to this, some Asians had established themselves on the coast and in the interior of Kenya as traders and petty merchants. When the British arrived, they found these merchants useful in marketing of their manufactured goods and encouraged more Indian traders to come and settle in Kenya, leading to the formation of the lower petty bourgeois class.

The upper petty bourgeois class, which only included Europeans at first but later some Asians and Africans, quickly recognised that its interests were best served by aligning with the colonialist ruling class. Thus they became class allies, first of the British ruling class and later, of the African comprador class.

At this stage, it is important to take a closer look at the class structure of Asian Kenyans within the economic and political framework of Kenya.

In each historical period, two main classes can be identified: the working class and the petty bourgeois class. Each class has pursued its own economic class interests and held hands with its class allies from other nationalities. However, the petty bourgeois Asian Kenyans have never been the dominant economic force.

Both these ruling classes, the colonialists and the comprador, have always used Asian Kenyans as "whipping boys" to hide their own economic dominance, exploitation and corruption.

Owing to their "group" oppression as a minority nationality, the various components of the Asian Kenyan petty bourgeois class tend to stick together on the basis of their nationality, languages and cultures.

The Asian Kenya lower petty bourgeoisie is made up of petty traders, merchants, technicians and professionals. By economic definition, they would normally identify with the interests of artisans and workers. But, in practice, out of fear and a sense of political insecurity, they often seek protection by looking up to the few, very rich members of the upper and the middle petty bourgeois Asian Kenyans.

Today, this lower petty bourgeois class of Asian Kenyan petty traders, merchants, technicians and professionals forms the majority of Asian Kenyans. And, although these Asian Kenyans took up Kenyan citizenship and renounced British citizenship in 1963, they have never been allowed to feel "secure" and at home in Kenya on the false premise that they are "milking the economy."

In reality, however, the real exploitative power has belonged to the big British financiers and industrialists of the earlier colonial period, and to the comprador class and multinationals of the later period.

It is imperative, therefore, not to condemn all the various economic strata of the Asian Kenya petty bourgeois class as allies of the ruling class. If they huddle together, it is because they seek strength in unity against their oppression as a nationality.

Indeed, when it comes to the main struggle of the classes (the big bourgeois against workers/peasants), a good number of the lower petty bourgeoisie, at the time of active struggle against imperialists, did in fact join hands with workers and peasants at the democratic level as well as at the underground level.

Furthermore, having distributed themselves geographically throughout the country, these lower petty bourgeois Asian Kenya had acquired a wider consciousness and awareness of the Kenyan situation. This particular factor greatly facilitated their alliances with workers and peasants.

Having identified the petty traders, merchants, technicians and professionals among Asian Kenyans as potential allies of workers and peasants, we come to the most important class – the Asian Kenyan working class.

Together with their supporters, these Asian Kenyan workers were, and are, the natural class allies of African peasants and workers. During the struggle, they joined hands with the African workers and peasants in resisting imperialist exploitation and oppression.

The first Asian Kenyan workers were contracted by the British to come and build the Kenya/Uganda railway. The British had tried and failed to recruit the indigenous Kenyans for the building of the "iron snake," as the Africans called it. The Indian workers or "coolies" did come but for economic reasons beyond their control.

It is significant that the British had looked to India for contracting the labourers without whom they could not possibly have built the railway. India had had a longer history of imperialist exploitation and the impoverished peasants and workers had been left without any form of subsistence. It was therefore easier to move them physically to another part of the world to serve the needs of imperialism within the international division of labour.

All these Asian workers left their beloved homeland for an unknown new home which offered them dignity through work, thousands of miles across the seas. And so began the first Asian "worker" settlement in Kenya.

They came without a penny but with a political understanding and experience more potent than gold. They brought with them a wealth of experience of militant class struggles. They came armed with the knowledge of the weapons of organisation and of the power of newspapers, handbills, newsletters, pamphlets and such other means of raising worker consciousness and of forging unity along class lines.

This legacy was to prove of tremendous importance to the working class that was soon to emerge in urban Kenya. It was to prove crucial in the formation of peasant/worker alliances and in the build-up of struggle against the forces of imperialism.

As it happened the railway, which became the symbol of imperialist power and which was built on the sweat and blood of Asian Kenyans and Africans, became also the harbinger of imperialist downfall. As the railway grew, so did the working class, and with it grew workers' grievances and sorrows which welded into iron resistance to imperialist rule and oppression.

The conditions of work on the railway were atrocious and even deadly. Horrific are the stories of the man-eating lions of Tsavo who came as marauders into the railway workers' camps, killing many. Then there was another killer, malaria, and other fatal diseases without adequate, if any, provision of medical facilities and sanitation, or worker's compensation. Many lost their lives working in dangerous and inhospitable conditions. Others were maimed and incapacitated for life.

According to statistics recorded by Makhan Singh, the great Kenyan worker and trade union leader, out of the 31,983 Indian workers who had been brought from India between 1896 and 1901 by the British, 2,493 died and 6,454 became incapacitated. This high figure of the dead and injured was a direct consequence of the abysmal conditions of work in building the railway and it explains the roots of militancy and anti-imperialist organisation among Asian Kenyan workers. Many returned home at the expiry of their contracts. Some 6,724 stayed on and formed the backbone of the Asian Kenya working class.

In the face of extreme exploitation from very long working hours, very poor, unhealthy and unsafe conditions of work and very low wages, these Asian Kenyan railway workers began to organise themselves to fight their employers. To achieve this, they formed the first trade union in Kenya, the Railway Workers' Union.

Later on, as the railway was extended, Africans too joined in as railway workers and became fellow trade unionists. The trade union movement began to spread to other industries and centres and flourished, becoming the pivotal centre not only for economic demands, but political activities too.

The solidarity between the Asian Kenyan and African workers began to show itself very clearly in joint strike actions and protests. In the first famous Railway Workers' Strike of 1900, it was the unity of the Asian Kenyan and African workers that became its backbone. From Mombasa, the strike soon spread to other centres.

The 1914 "united front" strike of several unions against poll tax and other grievances lasted for more than a week and forced the employers to meet the workers' demands. The colonial government became very frightened in the face of this new power of the workers based on organisation and unity and reacted by deporting the workers' leaders, including Mr. L. W. Ritch, Merchand Puri and Tirath Ram.

It was this alliance of Asian Kenyan and African workers/peasants along class lines that the British feared the most and tried their utmost to break it up. As a result of this fear, Makhan Singh, Harry Thuku and others were arrested and detained for their organisational and trade unionist activities.

However, the trade union movement had mass support and despite detentions and other acts of repression by the colonial authorities, it continued to nurture new leaders. Thus, when Harry Thuku was arrested and subsequently detained in 1922, the workers took to the streets in a protest demonstration led by Mary Muthoni Nyanjiru. The colonial police and gun wielding settlers at the nearby Norfolk Hotel fired on the unarmed workers and brutally massacred 150 of them. Makhan Singh mentions that at least four women were killed that day and Mary Muthoni Nyanjiru was among them. Many others were injured.

The Asian Kenyan and African workers joined hands also to bring out publications to politicise fellow workers and trade unionists against the foreign exploiters and to spread ideas of unity and class struggle. The workers' newspapers, newsletters, handbills, posters and word of mouth as means of spreading knowledge and information became a very powerful weapon in the ideological warfare against the imperialists.

In response to the worker newspapers, the settler community and the rich Asian Kenyans brought out their own newspapers to serve their own interests. Just as the settler newspapers were deeply influenced by the ruling class ideology from Britain and South Africa, the working class activists received their inspiration from other struggling people around the world, including India and other African countries.

The Ghadar Connection
The Asian Kenyan working class in Kenya was greatly influenced by the national struggles of the Asian people in India, Goa and elsewhere. Staunch working class activists such as Makhan Singh and Pio Gama Pinto were

not only influenced by the Indian and Goan people's struggles, but had also taken an active part in them. They brought with them first hand experiences and knowledge of the power of people's struggles. Indeed, Makhan Singh had been jailed in India and Pio Gama Pinto had had to flee from the Goan Portuguese government forces for his political activism.

Moreover, the militant Asian Kenyan workers had links with and learnt profound lessons from the revolutionary Ghadar Party which had bases in 22 countries around the world. The word "Ghadar" means "revolution." The Kenya activist, Sitaram Acharya, was the leader of the Ghadar Party in Kenya.

In this capacity, he had regular contact with the revolutionary movements in Canada, India and other parts of the world and circulated revolutionary and anti-imperialist material among the Party supporters in Africa. A British military officer recognised him as "the brains and the moving spirit of the whole of the anti-British movement in East Africa", without of course realising that Sitaram Acharya was "the brains" mainly because he had the support of the Ghadar movement abroad.

Without even the knowledge of Sitaram Acharya's connections with the Ghadar revolutionary movement, the British government quickly understood that he was a grave danger to their rule. In 1915, he was arrested and deported to India.

Upon his release, Sitaram returned to Kenya and started publishing *The Democrat*, a worker newspaper which also was considered too dangerous by the British authorities; Sitaram was once again arrested in 1930.

In 1915 Sitaram had got away comparatively lightly with detention. Other Asian Kenyan members of the Ghadar Party in Kenya were treated more brutally. By May 1916, some of them were court martialled, 3 had been shot,

2 hanged and 8 imprisoned for terms of 6 months to 14 years.

They were convicted of various crimes ranging from "possession of seditious publications", "assisting the enemy", spreading "false" intelligence and "alarmist" reports and such other reasons. In December 1915, Keshwal Divedi, Chief Clerk in the High Court, was sentenced to death by hanging for having in his house 2 letters from Sitaram Acharya and a collection of "seditious" newspaper clippings. L.M. Savle, another active organiser, was also sentenced to death for the same offence as that of Divedi.

The Ghadar Party stood for the real needs of oppressed people everywhere which is why it was so readily accepted by them. This central purpose for its existence was carried to all corners of the world through its publications.

The publishing of its weekly newspaper *Ghadar di Goonj* was one of the most significant events in the struggle of colonised people. It was a clarion call for revolution and helped to nurture a revolutionary consciousness in the minds of people wherever it reached them. Through this paper and its other publications such as handbills, pamphlets, handbooks and revolutionary songbooks, the Ghadar Party called for unity and revolution. This unity and thinking was to become the deadliest enemy of British imperialism.

Founded in 1913 by an Indian, Lala Hardayal, the Ghadar Party's main objective was to liberate India through an armed struggle and to establish a national government on the basis of equality and justice.
Lala Hardayal unfailingly pointed out the Party's policy of equality for all in which there was no room for the rich to exploit the poor. The Party was also internationalist in outlook and each of its members was honour bound to fight against slavery in all its forms.

Through the Indian working class, the Ghadar Party had a profound effect on the African working class movement and, through it, on the whole anti-imperialist struggle in Kenya. It was this legacy of the Ghadar Party's influence that was carried on to a national level from the Kenya Land and Freedom Army (the Mau Mau) by uncompromising fighters like Pio Gama Pinto, Makhan Singh and Ambubhai Patelll.

This background of the Ghadar Party and the Ghadar Movement throughout the world shows how important it was in arousing anti-imperialist feeling and in raising awareness of other people's struggles all over the world in the face of sharpening class contradictions. It made people aware of the nature of imperialism, imperialist rivalries, the ensuing world wars and victims of wars, resulting in further intensification of people's struggles.

It is not surprising therefore that the British colonial authorities were seriously concerned about the spread of the Ghadar Movement, not only in Kenya, but also throughout the world. It explains also why they reacted so severely when they uncovered the Ghadar Movement in Kenya.

The ideology of the Ghadar Party found expression through Asian Kenyan newspapers and publications. These were published in Gujarati, Punjabi, Hindi, Kiswahili and English.

The insistence of Asian Kenyan in promoting and proudly holding on to their nationality languages and cultures in their newspapers, in their homes and in their community schools, served as a profound lesson to other nationalities in their resistance to cultural imperialism.

One of the newspapers published in Kiswahili, The *Wahindi*, was started by an Indian, Chatrabh Bhat. His message of solidarity between the Asian Kenyan and African workers was considered a serious threat by the colonial government and he was deported to Tanganyika for his publishing activities.

This did not deter him and he continued publishing the paper, this time from Dar-es-Salaam.

Some of the other Asian Kenyan worker oriented newspapers were *The Chronicle*, started in 1960 by Goss, *Coast Guardian* started in 1919 and published and edited by Manilal A. Desai, *India Voice*, started in 1915 and published and edited also by Manilal A. Desai, and *India Voice of British East Africa, Uganda and Zanzibar*, started in 1911.

These early working class newspapers not only interpreted local events in their anti-imperialist and global working class context, but they also brought to their readers a larger awareness of the anti-imperialist struggles being waged in other parts of the world. This was an aspect that had been kept hidden from the colonised people in order to isolate them from world events.

For example, the *East African Chronicle*, published and edited by Manilal A. Desai, featured articles on the Sinn Fein in Ireland, on Gandhi in India and on Marcus Garvey in the Caribbean.

Besides featuring international issues, the *East African Chronicle* was directly involved in the Kenyan nationalist movement of the time. The paper published various African grievances over land, labour and wages policies. It also helped to print the articles and pamphlets in Kiswahili for Harry Thuku who distributed these to his fellow workers and trade unionists. Such activities led to frequent police harassment and raids on Desai's newspaper offices.

In addition, the settler press regularly attacked Manilal A. Desai and the *East African Chronicle* for the progressive stand they took on national issues and their local commitment and action to achieve working class victories.

Manilal A. Desai, however, continued to be an outspoken critic of colonial rule and turned the offices of *East African Chronicle* into a meeting place of Indian and African political activists. His newspaper had to close down after the arrest of Harry Thuku.

Today there stands in a corner of Tom Mboya Street of Nairobi the Desai Memorial Hall and the Desai Memorial Library, a fitting tribute to the man who devoted his life to the cause of anti-imperialist struggle.

By 1922 colonialism had entrenched itself and established its own industries to exploit Kenyan land, labour and other resources. This resulted in creating a large and powerful proletariat whose organisational skills increased as the struggle intensified.

While the western power rivalry for resources and markets intensified, so did class contradictions and people's resistance and struggles, reaching their peak by the end of World War II. By 1948, the resistance in Kenya had arrived at the level of armed struggle.

As the struggle heightened, so did British colonial repression. In response, worker organisations and publications found more sophisticated and underground forms of expression. They began to be more militant.

It was around 1935 that militant trade unions were established by Makhan Singh working with African colleagues. His contribution was enormous not only in terms of trade union movement but also in the overall liberation struggle. Under Makhan Singh, the unions started to publish handbills run off on typewriters and cyclostyled. This was cheaper and escaped censorship. Moreover, the unions could publish in as many as six languages to reach as wide an audience as possible. These languages included Kiswahili, Gikuyu, Gujarati, Urdu, Punjabi and English. By 1948, there were about 16 trade unions affiliated to the Labour Trade Union of East Africa, with a total membership of 10,000 workers.

As workers' publications and organisations lashed out more militantly, the settlers and their petty bourgeois allies began to panic and formed new organisations for "Home Rule" that were more acceptable to them. But, as the worker/peasant forces marched boldly ahead towards their own goals and their own preferred organisations, in 1952 the colonial authorities slapped down on the people the declaration of the State of Emergency.

Meanwhile, several prominent Asian Kenyan newspapers had emerged during this period which included the *Daily Chronicle*, the *Colonial Times* and the *Kenya Daily Mail*. The *Daily Chronicle,* said Oginga Odinga, was the first and only English language newspaper in Kenya to advocate a militant nationalist policy.

Pio Gama Pinto was the chief editor of the *Daily Chronicle* but he helped also with the preparation of Kenya African Union (KAU) memoranda and such other activities which led later on to the armed resistance of the Kenya Land and Freedom Army (Mau Mau) in which Pinto came to play an invaluable role.

G.L.Vidyarthi was another influential publisher and editor. His publications included the *Colonial Times* with its motto of "Free, Frank and Fearless Press." The paper lived up to its motto and resulted in a four-month jail sentence for its Chief Editor, G.L. Vidyarthi. In 1955, Vidyarthi also owned and co-edited a Kiswahili newspaper, *Habari*, which became a political paper and was charged for sedition by the British authorities.

In 1952, Vidyarthi started another Kiswahili newspaper, *Jicho* (Eye) which became extremely popular. *Jicho* was edited by Mr. Henry L. Gathigira who later on was to become Editor-in-Chief of *The Standard*. *Jicho* closed down in

1962 on the eve of independence.

Activists such as Pio Gama Pinto, Makhan Singh, Channan Singh, Haroon Ahmed and D.K. Sharda used the *Daily Chronicle* to support their activities at the East African Trade Union Congress as well as their nationalist, non-racial, anti-British worker oriented activities. Their political demand was "Independence Now" to be followed by development along socialist lines.

Whereas the *Daily Chronicle* stood for the united worker-peasant stand against imperialism and independence, the *Colonial Times* and the *Kenya Daily* Mail, which had been progressive at one time, began to represent the voices of those petty bourgeois Asian Kenyans who sided with the colonial point of view. These two latter newspapers had steadily regressed and become more reactionary by 1947.

Thus, just as the split between Asian Kenyan working class supporters and petty bourgeois colonial supporters became wider and more clearly defined, similar to that between the African workers and the African petty bourgeoisie, so did the stand taken by their various publications become more clearly defined and reflected their own specific interests.

The worker-peasant supporters who demanded complete independence were led by Makhan Singh and Pio Gama Pinto. Makhan Singh was, indeed, the first Kenyan in the history of Kenya's freedom struggle to make a public demand in 1950 for "complete independence and sovereignty" for East African colonies.

Makhan Singh, Pio Gama Pinto and their supporters were opposed not only by the British colonial government and settlers, but also by petty bourgeois Africans and Asian Kenyans. The latter included some Asian members of the Legislative Council who lost no opportunity to attack Makhan Singh as well as the *Daily Chronicle.* Like the British authorities, they also branded

Makhan Singh and Pio Gama Pinto as "communists" and accused them of "misleading" the labour movement in Kenya.

Govind D. Rawal, one of the editors of the *Daily Chro*nicle, clearly saw through these ruling elite tactics of dividing Asian Kenyan communities so that their energies would be spent in internal fights instead of uniting with their African class allies to fight colonialism. G.D. Rawal was fined and imprisoned for writing these truths in his paper.

Other Asian Kenyan newspapers set up by progressive Asian Kenyans included *Forward* (1946) and *Tribune* (1951-52), both of which stood for unity of Asians Kenyans and Africans, opposition to "kipande," elected representatives and equality in employment. *Tribune* was among the 50 Kenyan publications banned by the colonial government when it declared a State of Emergency in 1952.

Not only were the pages of such progressive newspapers open to the printing of articles from African nationalists and freedom fighters, but the Asian Kenyan printing press was responsible at the same time for the actual printing of the African newspapers and so contributed significantly to the growth of the Kenyan nationalist movement.

The lessons of organisation and communication, learnt from the above-mentioned forms of resistance and struggle, proved to be crucial later on in the armed struggle movement.

During this period of heightened activity, the number and quality of publications as well as demonstrations, boycotts, strikes and protests increased. No sooner were certain publications banned, new ones emerged to take their place.

The boycott of the government celebrations of the Charter Day, when Nairobi was given City Status in 1950 by the colonial authorities, became a national as well as a workers' protest. Makhan Singh, General Secretary of the East African Trade Union Congress, declared that there were "two Nairobis, that of the rich and that of the poor. The status of the latter Nairobi has not changed and there is nothing for us to celebrate."

The East African Trade Union Congress itself became a publisher in its own right and disseminated its own views through cyclostyled handbills and circulars in English, Kiswahili and Gujarati.

The victories won by workers and their organisations alarmed the settlers and their colonial government, making them panic. In order to break worker unity, they arrested Fred Kubai and Makhan Singh on 15 May 1950. Makhan Singh went on to spend altogether 15 years in detention. On 16 May 1950, the workers met and declared a general strike. The strikers demanded not only the release of Makhan Singh, Fred Kubai and other detainees, but also their economic and political rights.

This strike lasted till 24 May 1950 and spread to all the major towns, with more than a hundred thousand workers participating. It was widely supported by peasants and workers who donated food and cash to sustain the families of the striking workers.

Makhan Singh says "…the workers and their supporters had shown unprecedented courage and heroism in defying the colonial authorities and employers. It was a great general strike in the history of Kenya's trade union movement as well as the national movement."

While all this was going on, secret meetings were taking place where oaths were administered in preparation for eventual armed struggle. Bildad Kaggia refers to this period as one of great change where people were becoming impatient with pursuing fruitless constitutional methods to attain independence.

With the launching of the armed struggle, both overt and underground publishing activities proliferated.

Pio Gama Pinto was deeply involved in every aspect of the struggle for independence. As such he was in a better position to serve national interests through his publishing activities.

Bildad Kaggia makes special mention of Pinto's assistance to him and other African politicians in the form of private advice and practical help to run their own newspapers.

Ramogi Achieng Oneko mentions Pinto's contribution to the development of oral tradition for communication purposes in detention camps. Pinto's mentoring has also been mentioned by J.M. Kariuki, who was later on assassinated for his outspokenness and principled stand.

When Pinto went to New Delhi for discussions with Pandit Nehru, he asked for assistance to start a nationalist paper in Kenya. Pandit contributed towards the funds with which Pio Gama Pinto launched the Pan Africa Press Limited, which went on to publish *Sauti ya Mwafrika*, *Pan Africa* and the *Nyanza Times*.

Pio Gama Pinto remained a revolutionary in word and in action in the face of all hardships and hurdles. His outstanding political contribution and principled adherence to the aims and goals of the struggle, even after independence, were deeply resented and feared by those in power. Pio Gama Pinto had become a serious threat. Thus on the morning of Wednesday the 24th of February 1965, Pio Gama Pinto was assassinated outside his own gate as he left home. Like Kimathi, he died for his principles and for continuing his struggle for "total independence" of Kenya.

Oginga Odinga says:

"Pio Gama Pinto was a great Kenyan patriot. He leaves a gap in our political struggle for full freedom that few men – none that I know of – can fill... When the repression was launched against KAU, Pinto organised political defences. When fighting started from the forests, Pinto maintained political liaison and supplied arms and money to the freedom fighters from supply lines in Nairobi. When the (colonial) authorities caught up with his activities, he served his term of detention (seven years).

"When he was released and freed from restriction, he devoted himself to the campaign for the release of other detainees and for the support of their dependents. He was a brilliant organiser and a resourceful political leader. He threw himself into helping KANU win the 1961 elections, into founding our independent press, into the campaign for the East African Federation, into the struggle against imperialism..."

Another prominent Asian Kenyan publisher and activist who played a very important role in the struggle during this period was Ambubhai H. Patel. Armed with his qualifications as a book binder and his fierce anti-imperialist convictions, Ambubhai (as he was affectionately called), plunged into the publishing and political work organised by the Mau Mau.

During the Mau Mau period, Ambubhai contributed articles for the Mau Mau underground newspapers, helped actively to print them and even to distribute them. As an Asian Kenyan, he often evaded the colonial police and moved freely carrying messages and handbills to areas where others could not go.

For many years, Ambubhai and his wife, Lila Patel, gave refuge and shelter to

Margaret Kenyatta from colonial authorities.

At the Kapenguria trial, it was Ambubhai who, with the help of Pio Gama Pinto, managed to "borrow" from the court a copy of the Kapenguria judgement which had not been read out by the judge nor released officially. He reproduced 300 copies with the help of an Asian Kenyans typist, Shirin Meghji. Of these, he sent out 250 copies to leaders all over the world as the colonial government was not willing to let the world read the judgement.

Ambubhai also secretly collected photographs of Mau Mau freedom fighters which were to be the basis of a proposed pictorial record of "Daring Freedom Fighters of Kenya."

It should be noted that these prominent Asian Kenyan activists in the struggle only gained credibility with African people because they stood up for and acted in the interests of Kenyan workers and peasants. They had set themselves high standards for carrying out their work with dedication and enormous sacrifices.

At the same time, it should be pointed out that they were able to carry out their qualitative work mainly because they had active support teams of other Asian Kenyans working with them. There were support teams in legal, medical and many technical fields such as printing, gun-making and other areas requiring special skills.

Lawyers such as A.R. Kapila and D. N. Pritt (who was also the defence lawyer at the Kapenguria trial) and Fritz D'Souza, are some of those prominent people who worked devotedly and ceaselessly for detainees and for worker/peasant rights.

Doctors such as Yusuf Eraj and Dr. Singh gave free medical services and advice to freedom fighters, workers and peasants.

In the publishing field, people such as Channan Singh, Haroon Ahmed, Pranlal Seth, D.K. Sharda, and A.B. Patel contributed also towards funding, printing, editing and related services.

Other areas to be highlighted include the work of innumerable technicians and engineers who participated in teaching crafts and trades to other workers. Their knowledge and imparting of skills to their comrades proved to be crucial in the armed struggle. Jaswant Singh Bharaj, in particular, is well remembered for his contribution in training the Mau Mau in the craft of making guns and other weapons in factories set up in the forests and in the homes of partisans.

Mention should also be made of the Indian High Commissioner, Apa Pant, who was a progressive and who, with the knowledge and encouragement of the Indian government, secretly gave assistance to the freedom struggle.

In addition, there were other Asian Kenyan families, many and nameless, who lived in the strategic areas of Eastleigh and Pangani bordering Mathare Valley which was the centre of urban Mau Mau guerrilla activities. They secretly gave food, clothing, shelter and refuge to Mau Mau freedom fighters fleeing from the colonial police and militia. These families also helped in hiding guns and weapons of freedom fighters in trouble, or even delivered guns in the dead of night to the Mau Mau.

Many other Asian Kenyans also participated through making cash and material donations towards the cause of anti-imperialist struggle for Kenya's freedom.

The difference in objectives should be highlighted, however, in the struggle of those petty bourgeois Asian Kenyans who fought at the bourgeois democratic level within the framework of the imperialist constitution and the Legislative Council. They fought not to overthrow the yoke of imperialism but to get equal opportunities for Asian Kenyans and Africans, opportunities which only the settler class enjoyed. In this they served the limited goals and interests of their own petty bourgeois class.

Summing Up

In summing up, one particular note resonates and deserves special mention. And that is, the Asian Kenyans' influence (especially that of their working class) has been far in excess of their absolute numbers (once 150,000, now down to 60,000), only about 0.5% of Kenya's population at the time of writing this article (1987). This disproportionate influence in terms of their population percentage, can be put down to a mixture of factors.

Firstly, Asian Kenyans have been exposed to double oppression as a class and as a minority nationality far removed from their land of origin. This has given an edge to their consciousness and struggle.

Geographically, they have been distributed throughout the country and so have acquired a wider awareness of the Kenyan nationhood.

Historically, they had made contacts with revolutionary and progressive ideas and movements abroad and received news of the Indian struggle for independence on a regular basis.

They had experienced, at first hand, imperialist exploitation in India, Pakistan, Bangladesh, Sri Lanka and Goa, and were exposed to it for the second time in Africa. Thus they were quick to draw comparisons and apply appropriate lessons in class alliances and class struggle.

The example of Gandhi in South African resistance was an added inspiration for resisting oppression and colour bar at home in Kenya.

In the field of technology, they had acquired higher skills in the use of tools and machines which they were able to pass on to their fellow African workers.

Through use of Indian capital, they were able to acquire machinery (such as printing presses) for themselves, instead of having to depend on the availability and censorship of imperialist capital. They could make use of such machinery as printing presses for the production of publications in defiance of the colonialists.

As in other countries, the colonialists had denied them access to land in Kenya, thereby restricting their options for survival. They had to turn instead to higher education and better skills and professions. These were usually acquired overseas where they came into contact with ideas of resistance and liberation.

Even petty bourgeois traders saw the necessity of their children acquiring higher education to overcome economic insecurity.

Asian Kenyans continued to have strong cultural ties with their country of origin. Holding on to their languages and way of life was a means of cultural resistance to imperialism. Moreover, it kept intact their community ties with each other and with other Asian Kenyan communities in Kenya and in their various homelands abroad.

Indian films such as "Jansi Ki Rani" (Queen of Jansi), a story of a queen leading her warrior army in armed combat with British forces in India, had tremendous impact on the worker struggle in Kenya. In retaliation, the British promptly banned it from being distributed and shown in cinemas.

After the ban was imposed, many Asian Kenyans made the long and arduous journey to Tanganyika to watch it. It is interesting to note that in the New India Army led by Subhas Chandra Bose, one of India's great freedom fighters, a special brigade for women had been formed in India called the Jansi Ki Rani Brigade.

Asian Kenyans continued to hold on ferociously to their various languages, songs, dances and traditions under all circumstances. This action in itself was anti-imperialist in nature for it rejected the wholesale embrace of imperialist cultural forms of languages, dances, music and songs in lieu of their own.

The Asian Kenyan's struggle to have their own independent schools, the eventual establishment of these schools with their own syllabuses which gave prominence to their own languages and history, pushed forward with a leap their struggle against cultural imperialism.

All the above aspects contributed to the particular contributions of Asian Kenyans to the anti-imperialist struggle in Kenya. Since they had the same class interests and aspirations as the Kenyan workers and peasants, their battles had the common and united aim to achieve economic as well as political freedom from the imperialist stranglehold.

Unfortunately, Asian Kenyans have been lumped together by the ruling classes as one homogeneous class. This camouflaging of class differences is done subtly and deliberately to hide from the people the real contradictions and the nature of the class struggle. It clouds the knowledge of who are the enemies and who are the allies.

The British colonialists were fully aware that once class struggle and class alliances were understood by the people, it would become easier for them to grasp who was the enemy and the perpetrator of their woes. Battle lines could then become clear cut and drawn for the real struggle against imperialism and neo-colonialism.

Eventually, when armed struggle heightened in the late 1950s and 1960s, the imperialists realised they could no longer stay on as direct rulers. They had to quit but only after they had forged class alliances with the nascent petty bourgeois Africans who had the same aspirations as theirs for individual rather than social gain.

This alliance led to the emergence of the comprador class which took over the political reins intent on owning the power and financial rewards that come with it while leaving the economic reins in the hands of the imperialists. Thus the colonialists continued to exert and enjoy their economic control under the chameleon cloak of neo-colonialism. It is noteworthy that many of those who became part of the new comprador class had once belonged to the infamous "Home Guard" colonial brigade.

On the international scene, while western power rivalry for supremacy continued, US imperialism upstaged and pushed out British imperialism from the front line in Kenya, as indeed elsewhere in the world, after the Second World War. For the majority of the Kenyan people this change made no difference; it was merely the Changing of the Guard. People's exploitation and economic dependence continued under new guises.

However, as history continues to show, while new and more sophisticated forms of imperialism and subjugation emerged, exploitation and oppression also became subtler and reached new heights. This in turn sharpened further the contradictions and people's struggles adopted reciprocal and newer forms of resistance.

In conclusion, the aim of this brief article has been to highlight and present an overview, albeit very briefly, of the significant role played by Asian Kenyans in the Kenyan struggle for independence. The most outstanding among them were Makhan Singh and Pio Gama Pinto. Both these leaders worked selflessly and devotedly throughout their life for the struggle, were highly respected by the people and had a revolutionary and transformative impact on the Kenyan struggle. It is high time that Asian Kenyans take ownership of their history and take justifiable pride in the glorious participation of Asian Kenyans in the freedom struggle of Kenya.

નઝમી દૂરાણી: ઐતિહાસિક અવલોકન

એશિયન કેન્યાવાસીઓએ મોટી સંખ્યામાં આ દેશને પોતાની જન્મભૂમિ તરીકે અપનાવવાની શરૂઆત કરી, તેને નજીકમાં ૧૦૦ વરસ થશે. એટલે આ સમય અનૂકૂળ કહેવાય કે આપણે જરા આપણા ઈતિહાસ તરફ નજર નાખીએ. આપણા બાપ-દાદાઓ શા માટે પોતાની માતૃભૂમિનો ત્યાગ કરી એક નવા સ્વદેશની શોધમાં નીકળી પડ્યા ?

આમ તો પૂર્વ આફ્રિકા અને ભારત વચ્ચેનો સંબંધ હજારો વરસોનો છે. આ સંપર્કનું કારણ હતો વેપાર. હિંદી મહાસાગરના માર્ગ દ્વારા આફ્રિકા અને એશિયા વચ્ચે ઘણી સદીઓથી વેપાર ચાલી રહ્યો હતો. આ સંબંધને કારણે થોડા ઘણા ભારતીયોએ આ ખંડના કાંઠાના વિસ્તારમાં

વસાહતો થોડી સંખ્યામાં ઊભી કરી હતી. આવી જ રીતે થોડા ઘણા આફ્રિકી લોકોએ પણ ભારતના જુદા જુદા ભાગોમાં વસાહત કરેલ. આ લોકોના વંશ આજે પણ જોવામાં આવે છે કે જેઓ સીદીઓ તરીકે ઓળખાય છે.

આ ઘણા લાંબા ગાળાનો સંબંધ ૧૬મી સદીમાં પોર્ચુગીઝ સામ્રાજ્યશાહીઓએ બળજબરીથી બંધ કરાવ્યો. આની સાથે આ બે ખંડોની મલિકત મોટી કલમે અહીંના દેશોમાંથી નીકળી યુરોપ લઈ જવામાં આવી. ૧૭મી સદીના અંતમાં પોર્ચુગીઝ સામ્રાજ્ય શાહીઓનો જોરદાર હથિયારબંધ સામનો થવાને કારણે હાર થઈ અને હદી મહાસાગર પરનો તેઓનો કબજો તૂટી ગયો. આ સાથે પૂર્વ આફ્રિકા, અરબસ્તાન અને ભારતના પશ્ચિમિ વસ્તિાર વચ્ચેનો જૂનો સંબંધ ફરી ચાલુ થયો. ભારતથી આવતા વેપારીઓ અને ખલાસીઓમાં વધારે પડતા ગુજરાત પુરાંતના માણસો હતા.

પરંતુ આ સંબંધ પાછો વધારે ન વધી શક્યો કારણ કે આ દરમ્યાન એક નવી હુમલાખોર સત્તા અહીં દાખલ થઈ. આ વખતે આ શાંત સંપર્ક તોડવાવાળા હતા અંગ્રેજ સામ્રાજ્યવાદીઓ. તેઓએ પહેલાં ભારતના પૂર્વના વસ્તિાર ઉપર બળજબરીથી કબજો કર્યો. ત્યાંથી આસ્તે આસ્તે આખા દેશ પર કબજો જમાવ્યો, અનેક શૂરવીરોએ તેઓનો સામનો કર્યો અને શહીદી વહોરી લીધી.

૧૯મી સદીમાં ગુલામોનો વેપાર બંધ કરવાના બહાને અંગ્રેજ સામ્રાજ્યશાહીઓએ પૂર્વ આફ્રિકા ઉપર હુમલો કરવાનું શરૂ કર્યું અને આ સદીના અંતમાં અહીં પણ પોતાનો લશ્કરી કબજો જમાવ્યો. આ સિવાય અંગ્રેજોનો કબજો દુનિયાના બીજા ઘણા ભાગોમાં પણ ફેલાએલ.

પૂર્વ આફ્રિકામાં જે ભારતીઓની વસાહત ૧૯મી સદીમાં થયેલ તે અંગ્રેજ સામ્રાજ્યના બીજા ભાગોમાં થયેલ વસાહતનો એક જ ભાગ છે. દાખલા તરિકે ૧૮૩૪ પછી અંગ્રેજ હકુમત નીચેના વેસ્ટઈન્ડઝિના મુલકો જેવા કે જમાઈકા, ટ્રીનીદાદ, ગુયાના વગેરેમાં ઘણા ભારતીઓને શેરડીના મોટા ખેતરોમાં કામ કરવા લઈ જવામાં આવેલ. આ સિવાય દક્ષણિ આફ્રિકા, મોરેશયિસ, ફીજી અને બીજા ઘણા મુલકોમાં મજૂરોને લઈ જવામાં આવેલ.

દેખાવમાં તો આ મજૂરો પોતાની બનિ-દબાણ મરજીથી કરારનામા ઉપર સહી કરી પરદેશ લઈ જવામાં આવ્યા. પરંતુ બે નોખી જાતના દબાણ આ લોકો પર હતા. ઘણા જેઓ શહેરોમાં નોકરીની શોધમાં આવ્યા હોય તેઓને ઘણી ગોરી કંપનીઓ બળજબરીથી પકડી અને સહી કરાવતી અથવા તો ખોટી વાત કરી અને છેતરીને સહી કરાવતા. બીજી બાજુ ઘણા માણસોની આર્થિક સ્થતિએિવી કફોડી હતી કે પરદેશ કમાવા ગયા વગર બીજો કોઈ છૂટકો જ ન હતો. આવી સ્થતિના કારણો આપણે નીચે વધારે વગિતવાર તપાસશું.

અંગ્રેજ સામ્રાજ્યના બીજા મુલકોમાં આવા કરારનામી મજૂરોની હાલત અને ૧૫થી ૧૭મી સદી સુધી જે આફ્રિકી ગુલામોને બળજબરીથી લઇ જવામાં આવેલ તેઓની હાલતમાં ઘણો ફેર ન હતો. આ મજૂરોની જિંદગી તેઓના ગોરા શેઠ્યાના હાથમાં હતી. દિવસના ૨૦ કલાક સુધી કામ કરાવવું. મનમાં ફાવે ત્યારે તેઓને કીરૂરતાથી માર મારવો, પોતાના છુટ્ટીના વખતમાં પણ તેઓને રજા નહી કે જ્યાં જવું હોય ત્યાં જઇ શકે અથવા તો મન ફાવતું કરી શકે. છ છ મહિનાઓ સુધી પગારના પૈસા રોકી રાખવા, આવી વર્તણૂક સામે તેઓને ફરિયાદ કરવાનો અધિકાર પણ નહીં.

પૂર્વ આફ્રિકામાં આવા જ કરારનામામાં સહી કરાવી ભારતીય મજૂરોને કેન્યા-યુગાન્ડા વચ્ચેની રેલ બનાવવા માટે લાવવામાં આવ્યા. ૧૮૯૬થી ૧૯૩૦ના વરસો દરમ્યાન લગભગ ૩૨,૦૦૦ મજૂરો અહીં આવ્યા. આમાંથી ૨,૫૦૦ જેટલા માણસો અકસ્માત, બીમારી કે બીજા કારણોસર મૃત્યુ પામ્યા. બીજા ૬,૫૦૦ કામ કરતા ઇજા થતા પાછા ઘર ભેગા કરી દેવામાં આવેલ. ૧૬,૦૦૦થી ઉપર મજૂરો કરારનો વખત કે કામ પૂરૂં થતાં પાછા ચાલ્યા ગયા, અને ૬,૭૦૦ માણસોએ પૂર્વ આફ્રિકામાં રહી જવાનું નક્કી કર્યું.

આ સિવાય થોડા ઘણા વેપારીઓની તેમ જ તેઓની પેઢીઓમાં નોકરી કરવાવાળાની વસાહત તો અહીં પહેલેથી હતી. જો કે આ પેઢીઓ તો કિનારાના ગામોમાં હતી પરંતુ ધંધાના કારણે આ લોકોનું પૂર્વ આફ્રિકાના અંદરના ઇલાકામાં અવર-જવર તો ચાલુ જ હતી. ગઇ સદીના છેલ્લા દાયકા દરમ્યાન આ વેપાર વધવા લાગ્યો. ભારતીય વેપારી પેઢીઓનો ધંધો વધારવાને કારણે બીજા માણસો અહીં આવ્યા. આ સાથે બીજા ઘણા માણસો કે જેઓની આર્થિક સ્થિતિ સારી ન હતી તેઓએ થોડા ઘણા પૈસાની બચત કરી પોરબંદર, કરાંચી કે મુંબઇથી વહાણની સફર કરી પૂર્વ આફ્રિકા કામની શોધમાં આવ્યા.

ઉપરના અહેવાલથી સવાલ એ ઊભો થાય છે કે ૧૯મી સદીમાં ભારતની એટલે કે અત્યારના ભારત, પાકિસ્તાન અને બંગલા દેશની હાલત કેવી હતી કે જેના કારણસર પોતાની માતૃભૂમિનો ત્યાગ કરી લાખો વતનીઓ હજારો માઇલની સફર કરી. દુનિયાના અનેક ભાગોમાં જઇ અને આ અજાણ્યા મુલકોમાં વસાહત કરી? આમ કરતાં અનેક લોકો માર્યા ગયા અને બીજાઓએ ઘણા દુઃખો સહન કરી આ નવા મુલકોને અપનાવ્યા. શું પોતાની જન્મભૂમિમાં તેઓની હાલત આ બધાં દુઃખો અને મોત કરતાં પણ ખરાબ હતી ?

આ સવાલનો જવાબ આપવા માટે આપણને અંગ્રેજ સામ્રાજ્યશાહી નીચેના ભારતના ઇતિહાસ તરફ નજર નાખવી પડશે.

સૌજન્ય : "અલક મલક", જૂન ૧૯૮૬; પૃ. ૦૯-૧૦.

- ૨ -

આ પહેલાં, આપણે એ સવાલ રજૂ કરેલ કે ગઈ સદીમાં અંગ્રેજ સામ્રાજ્ય નીચેના ભારતની આર્થિક સ્થિતિ કેવી હતી કે જેના કારણે લાખો ભારતીઓ પોતાની માતૃભૂમિ છોડી દુનિયાના બીજા ભાગોમાં પોતાનું નવું રહેઠાણ બનાવ્યું?

૧૭૫૭થી ૧૮૫૭ સુધીની સદી દરમ્યાન અંગ્રેજોના રાજનું સાધન ઈસ્ટ ઈન્ડિયા કંપની (કંપની સરકાર) હતી. ૧૮૫૭માં દેશપ્રેમીઓએ બળવો પોકાર્યો અને પરદેશી શાસન સત્તાને ખતમ કરવાની કોશિશ કરી. બે વરસથી વધારે લડાઈ ચાલુ રહ્યા બાદ દેશભક્તોની હાર થઈ. ત્યાર બાદ દેશનો કબજો અંગ્રેજ સરકારે સીધો પોતાના હાથમાં લીધો. આ કબજો, પછી ૧૯૪૭ સુધી ચાલ્યો. આ વરસો દરમ્યાન અંગ્રેજોએ ભારતીઓની એકતા તોડવા માટે તેઓમાં અનેક ભેદભાવો ઊભા કર્યા. ખાસ કરીને હિંદુ-મુસલમાનો વચ્ચે ખટપટ ઊભી કરી. ૧૮૫૭ની પહેલી આઝાદીના જંગમાંથી તેઓએ પાઠ શીખ્યા કે આ બન્ને કોમો જો સાથે મળીને લડે તો તેઓનું સામ્રાજ્ય જલદીથી ખતમ થઈ જશે. દાખલા તરીકે આ લડાઈના નેતાઓમાં નીચે મુજબના સરદારોનો સમાવેશ હતો : મંગળ પાંડે, આહમદ શાહ, લક્ષ્મીબાઈ (ઝાંસીની રાણી), બહાદુર શાહ ઝફર (મુઘલ બાદશાહ), તાત્યા ટોપે.

આવી એકતાના બીજા અનેક દાખલાઓ આપણને ભારતના ઈતિહાસમાં મળે છે. આ સદીની શરૂઆતમાં જ્યારે અંગ્રેજોએ બંગાળના હિંદુ અને મુસલમાનોના વસિતારોના ભાગલા કરવાનું ઠરાવ્યું ત્યારે આ કોમોએ સાથે મળી તેનો જોરદાર સામનો કર્યો. રવીન્દ્રનાથ ટાગોર, અબ્દુલ રસૂલ, સુરેન્દ્રનાથ બેનરજી વગેરેની આગેવાની નીચે બંગાળીઓએ સ્વદેશી આંદોલન ઉપાડ્યું. 'વંદે માતરમ'નો નારો પોકારી વિદેશી માલનો બહિષ્કાર કર્યો. આ જોરદાર વિરોધની સામે અંગ્રેજોને લાચાર થઈ ભાગલાની નીતિ છોડવી પડેલ.

આવો એક બીજો દાખલો આ સદીના બીજા દાયકા દરમ્યાનના પંજાબમાં જોવા મળે છે. દેશભરમાં આ વખતે પરદેશી શોષણ અને અત્યાચારો વિરોધી ઝુંબેશ ચાલી રહી હતી. ૧૯૧૯માં ડૉ. કીચલુ અને ડૉ. સત્યપાલની નેતાગીરી હેઠળ પંજાબના હિંદુ, શીખ અને મુસલમાન લોકો કોઈ પણ ભેદભાવ વગર આ ઝુંબેશને આગળ વધારવા હડતાલો અને મોરચાઓ રચતા અને 'હિંદુ-મુસલમાન કી જય'ના નારા પોકારતા. આવી એકતા જોઈ, ડરી જઈ જુલમગાર સરકારી ફોજે જલિયાંવાલા બાગમાં બિનહથિયારી લોકો ઉપર બંદૂકથી હુમલો કર્યો. આ હુમલામાં એક હજારથી વધારે દેશભક્તો શહીદ થયા અને બીજા હજારો ઘાયલ થયેલ.

આવાં તો કેટલાંએ કિસ્સાઓ આપણને ઇતિહાસમાં જોવા મળે છે. દેશપ્રેમીઓની આવી એકતાને તોડવા ગોરાઓએ પૂરજોર ઝુંબેશ ઉપાડી અને અનેક ભેદભાવો ઊભા કર્યા. આમાં તેઓ સફળ થયા અને અંતે ૧૯૪૭માં દેશના બે ભાગલા થયા.

ભારત ઉપરના ૨૦૦ વરુષના પરદેશી શાસન સત્તાના રાજ દરમ્યાન એક ચીજ એવી હતી કે જેમાં જરા પણ ફેર નહતો. પડેલ-દેશ ઉપરનું શોષણ અનેક રીતે દેશની મલિકતને હાથ કરી પોતાના દેશ ભેગી કરી દેવી. ભારત ઉપર લશ્કરી હુમલો કરી અનેક દેશભક્તોને લડાઈમાં હરાવી અંગ્રેજોએ દેશ ઉપર કબજો જમાવ્યો. પરંતુ આ કબજો કરવા માટે જે ખર્ચો થયો તે ભારતવાસીઓ પાસેથી જ કઢાવ્યો. ૧૯મી સદીના પહેલાં ૩૦ વરુષ દરમ્યાન સામ્રાજ્યશાહીઓએ દેશને ૭૦ કરોડ પાઉન્ડની રકમ આપવાની ફરજ પાડી. દર વરસે ભારતને એક મોટી રકમ અંગ્રેજ સરકારને ભરપાઈ કરવી પડતી અને જો કોઈ કારણસર આ ભરપાઈ ના થઈ તો તેના ઉપર ૧૨% ચક્રવૃદ્ધિ વ્યાજ (કમ્પાઉન્ડ ઇન્ટરેસ્ટ) ભરવું પડે. દાખલા તરીકે ૧૯૦૧-૧૯૦૨ના વરુષ દરમ્યાન આ વ્યાજની રકમ ૧ કરોડ ૭૦ લાખ પાઉન્ડ(૧૭,૦૦૦,૦૦૦)ની હતી.

અંગ્રેજ સામ્રાજ્ય ભારતમાં સ્થાપિત થયું તે પહેલાં સેંકડો વરસોથી ભારતની કામગીરી અને હાથઉદ્યોગની વસ્તુઓ દુનિયાભરમાં પ્રખ્યાત હતી. પોતાનાં કારખાનાંઓમાં બનેલી વસ્તુઓને ઉત્તેજન આપવા માટે અંગ્રેજોએ ભારતના ઉદ્યોગોનો નાશ કર્યો. કારીગરો તેમ જ હાથઉદ્યોગ ચલાવનારાને સામ્રાજ્ય સરકારને કર ભરવાની ફરજ પડી, તેઓને હુકમ કરવામાં આવ્યો કે તેઓ શાસનસત્તાના કારભારી દ્વારા જ માલ વેચે અને તે પણ એકદમ નીચેના ભાવે. જો હુકમનું જરા પણ પાલન ના થયું તો કારખાનાંઓ બાળી નાખવામાં આવે, કારીગરોના હાથ કાપી નાખવામાં આવે અથવા તેઓની જાન પણ લઈ લેવામાં આવે. આવી વર્તણૂકને કારણે લાખો માણસો કામ વગરના થઈ ગયા.

ખેડૂતોની હાલત પણ અંગ્રેજોના રાજમાં આવી જ કફોડી થયેલ. પરદેશી સરકારે જમીન ઉપર એકદમ જ ઊંચો કર (લગામ) મૂક્યો. પાક સારો હોય કે ખરાબ, ખેડૂતે સરકારને કર તો ભરવો જ પડે. અગાઉના વખતમાં સારો પાક નીકળે તો તેઓ થોડો એક બાજુ રાખી મૂકે કે જે કોઈ વરસે સારો પાક ના ઉતરે ત્યારે કામ આવે. હવે તો એક પાકથી બીજો પાક ઉતરે તે દરમ્યાન પણ સાંસા પડવા લાગ્યા. સરકારને કર ના ભરાય તો તે ખેતરની લીલામી કરે. કર ભરવા માટે મોટે વ્યાજે પૈસા ઉધાર લેવા પડે અને તે પાછા ના ભરાય તો વ્યાજખાઉ જમીન જપ્ત કરી લે આવી હાલતમાં લાખો ખેડૂતો જમીન વગરના થઈ ગયા.

દેશમાં ભૂખમરો પણ વધી ગયો. ૧૭મી સદીના પહેલાં ૫૦ વરસમાં દેશના નોખા નોખા ભાગોમાં 7 વખત દુકાળ થયેલ કે જેમાં ૫ લાખ માણસો મારયા ગયા. આની સરખામણી આપણે

123

આ જ સદીના છેલ્લા ૫૦ વરસ સાથે કરીએ તો જોવા મળે છે કે આ વરસો દરમ્યાન ૨૪ વખત દુકાળ પડેલ આમાં ૨ કરોડ (૨૦,૦૦૦,૦૦૦) માણસો ભૂખે મરી ગયેલ.

જમીન વગરના ખેડૂતો ગામો તરફ કામની શોધમાં આકર્ષાયા, પરંતુ અહીં પરદેશી સરકારે દેશી ઉદ્યોગનો નાશ કરેલ શહેરોમાં પણ કામ મળવું મુશ્કેલ હતું. એટલે જો દેશ બહાર સુધારવાની આશા હોય તો તે તરફ ખેંચાઈ એ તો સ્વાભાવિક છે. આવું ખેંચાણ અંગ્રેજ સામ્રાજ્યના બીજા વસ્તારોમાંથી આવ્યું.

સૌજન્ય : "અલક મલક", જુલાઈ ૧૯૮૬; પૃ. ૦૯-૧૦.

- ૩ -

૧૮મી સદીના છેલ્લા ભાગમાં, અંગ્રેજો પોતાનું ઉત્તર અમેરીકાનું સામ્રાજ્ય ખોઈ બેઠેલા. આની સાથે તેઓએ પોતાની ખેતીવાડીની વસાહતો પણ ગુમાવી. પરંતુ ૧૯મી સદીના પહેલા ભાગમાં ફ્રાન્સ સાથે લડાઈમાં તેઓની જીત થતાં, ફ્રાન્સના જૂના ટાપુ સામ્રાજ્ય ઉપર કબજો જમાવ્યો અને ત્યાં મોટી કલમે વેચવા માટેના પાકો (દા.ત. શેરડી) પેદા કરવાનું નક્કી કર્યું, પણ આ ઈલાકાઓમાં મજૂરોની કમી હોવાને કારણે ભારતથી કરારનામી મજૂરોને લઈ જવામાં આવ્યા. આ સદીની અંતમાં જ્યારે તેઓએ દક્ષિણ અને પૂર્વ આફ્રિકા ઉપર કબજો વધારે જોરદાર બનાવ્યો ત્યારે અહીં પણ ભારતથી વસાહતીઓને લાવ્યા.

પૂર્વ આફ્રિકામાં જે ભારતીયો આવ્યા. તેઓ બે વર્ગના હતા. કરારનામી મજૂરો કે જેઓ રેલ બનાવવા લાવવામાં આવ્યા, અને બીજા વેપારીઓ અને તેઓની પેઢીઓમાં નોકરી કરવા વાળાઓ જેમ જેમ તેઓનો કબજો વધારે મજબૂત થતો ગયો તેમ તેમ રાજ્ય કારભાર વધતો ગયો. અંગ્રેજ વસાહતો એ ખેતીવાડીની ફળદ્રુપ જમીન આફ્રિકી હકદારો પાસેથી જપ્ત કરી. ગામો અને શહેરોનો વધારો થયો. આ સાથે અનેક કારીગરોની જરૂર ઊભી થઈ. એટલે ભારતથી સુથારો, ઈજનેરો, લુહારો, કડિયા, રંગારાઓ, દરજીઓ, મોચીઓ વગેરે આવ્યા. સરકારમાં બેંકોમાં એની વેપારી પેઢીઓ માટે કારકુનો, હિસાબનીસો વગેરેની જરૂર પડતાં થોડાં ઘણાં અંગ્રેજી ભણેલા માણસોને પણ અહીં આવવાનું ઉત્તેજન અપાયું. આ સાથે શિક્ષકો, વકીલો અને ડૉક્ટરોને લાવવામાં આવ્યા અથવા તો અહીંના ભારતીય વસાહતોના બાળકોને આવી કેળવણી આપવા માટે ઉત્તેજન આપ્યું.

પણ અંગ્રેજ સરકારે વધારે ઉત્તેજન તો વેપારી વર્ગને આપ્યું. સામ્રાજ્યશાહીઓને ખપતું હતું કે ભારતીય વેપારીઓ અને તેઓના નોકરિયાતો દેશના એક એક ખૂણામાં જઈ વેપાર

HISTORY

એતિહાસિક અવલોકન

નજમી રામજી   10-05-2016

'કેન્યાનું સૌ પ્રથમ ગુજરાતી અને અંગ્રેજી માસિક' –ની ઘોષણા સાથે "અલક મલક" સામયિક કેન્યાના પાટનગર નાઇરોબીથી 1985-86ના અરસામાં આરંભાયેલું. સામયિકના માનદ્ તંત્રી તરીકે પંકજ પટેલ હતા. જ્યારે માનદ્ સહતંત્રી તરીકે રશ્મિ પટેલ હતા. તેનું સંચાલન અશ્વિન ડી. શાહ (વિક્કી શાહ) તેમ જ જે.કે. મુટુરી કરતા. તો મુદ્રણ સ્થળ 'આર્ટીસ્ટીક પ્રિન્ટર્સ' હતું તેમ કહેવાયું છે.

આ સામિયકમાં નજમી રામજી નામના એક અભ્યાસુ લેખકની કલમે કટાર આવતી. વિક્ટોરિયા સરોવર કાંઠે આવેલા કિસુમુ ખાતે 31 માર્ચ 1942ના રોજ જન્મેલા આપણા આ નજમુદ્દીન દૂરાણીનું એક અકસ્માતમાં નાઇરોબીમાં 01 જુલાઇ 1990ના દિવસે કારમું અવસાન થયેલું. નજમીભાઇએ ગુજરાતી કિસ્વાહિલી અને અંગ્રેજીમાં ય લખાણ કર્યા છે. ખોજા પરિવારના આ નબીરાનું અવસાન થયા પછી, ગુજરાતી આલમે આ ઇતિહાસ ખોયો હોય, તેમ હાલ અનુભવાય છે.

નજમી રામજી 'ડિસેમ્બર ટ્વેલ્વ મૂવમેન્ટ' નામક ભુગર્ભ પ્રવૃત્તિમાં ય સક્રિયપણે સંકળાયેલા હતા અને કવિતા સર્જન ઉપરાંત પત્રકારત્વ ય કરતા રહેતા. વળી કેટલાંક સામયિકોનું પણ એ સંચાલન કરતા.

'નજમી રામજી' નામે લખતા, નજમુદ્દીન દૂરાણી વિશેની આ વિગતો અને આ સમગ્ર લેખન સામગ્રી એમના નાના ભાઇ શિરાજ દૂરાણીના સૌજન્યે પ્રાપ્ત થઇ છે. સહ્રદય આભાર.

....

તેઓને બે બાજુથી ફાયદો થાય. એક બાજુ આફ્રિકી જનતામાં પૈસાથી ખરીદાયેલ વસ્તુઓની માંગ વધે. રોકડની જરૂર પડતાં આફ્રિકી મજૂરો અંગ્રેજ વસાહતોનાં ખેતરોમાં કામ કરવા નીકળી પડે. બીજી બાજુ વેપારીઓ પોતાની દુકાનોમાં અંગ્રેજ કારખાનાંઓમાં બનાવેલી ચીજો

વેચે, આ ચીજો વિલાયતથી અંગ્રેજ આગબોટમાં પૂર્વ આફ્રિકા પહોંચે, આ માલનો વીમો ઉતરે અંગ્રેજ વીમાકંપનીઓમાં, ધંધામાં જે પૈસા આ વેપારીઓ કમાય તે જમા થાય અંગ્રેજ બેંકોમાં, એટલે બધી તરફથી નફો તો છેલ્વે બાકી અંગ્રેજ મૂડીદારોને જ મળે. પરંતુ અજાણ્યા મુલકમાં વેપાર કરવાનાં જે કષ્ટ અને જોખમ હોય તે ભારતીય વેપારીઓ ઉપાડે.

આ રીતે અંગ્રેજ શાસન સત્તાએ પૂર્વ આફ્રિકા અને દુનિયાના બીજા ભાગોમાં જ્યાં પોતાનો કબજો હતો તેવા મુલકો અને ત્યાંની પ્રજાના શોષણમાં ભારતીય વસાહતોનો ઉપયોગ કર્યો. આ સિવાય બીજી પણ ઘણી રીતે આ પ્રજાઓનું શોષણ કર્યું અને તેઓ ઉપર અત્યાચારો કર્યા. દાખલા તરીકે જેમ ભારતમાં તેઓએ બળજબરીથી મોટી કલમે લગામ એકઠી કરી અને રૈયતને પાયમાલ કરી નાખી તેવી જ રીતે કેન્યાની પ્રજા ઉપર ઘર દીઠ એક કર મૂક્યો (અંગ્રેજીમાં જે 'હટ ટેક્સ' તરીકે ઓળખાતો). ગઈ સદીની અંતમાં અને આ સદીની શરૂઆતમાં કોઈ પણ બહાને ગોરાઓ દેશના ખેડૂતો અને ભરવાડો પાસેથી લાખોના હિસાબે ગાયો અને બકરાંઓ જપ્ત કરેલ. આ ઉપરાંત દેશની ફળદ્રુપ જમીનના લાખો એકરો ઉપર કબજો કરી અને તેના અસલી માલિકોની હાલત આ જ જમીન ઉપર ગુલામો જેવી કરી નાખેલ.

કેન્યા અને ભારતની પરદેશી હકૂમત દરમ્યાનની સ્થિતિમાં ઘણું સરખાપણું જોવામાં આવે છે. આ ખાલી અંગ્રેજ સામ્રાજ્યશાહીની શોષણ અને જુલમમાં જ નહિ, પણ આવા શાસન સામે જે બળવો રચવામાં આવેલ તેમાં પણ જોવામાં આવે છે.

ભારતમાં તાત્યા ટોપે અને ઝાંસીની રાણી લક્ષ્મીબાઈ, ખુદીરામ બોઝ અને અશફાક ઉલ્લાખાન, ચંદ્રશેખર આઝાદ અને ભગત સહિ, સુભાષચંદ્ર બોઝ અને તેના સાથીદારો શાહનવાઝ ખાન અને લક્ષ્મીબાઈ, સ્વામીનાથન અને બીજાં અનેક લડવૈયાઓએ પરદેશી હુમલાખોરોનો હથિયારબંધ સામનો કરેલ. તેવી જ રીતે કેન્યામાં પણ અનેક દેશભક્તોએ ફિરંગીઓનો વિરોધ કરવા શસ્ત્રર ઉપાડેલ. તેઓના અમુક સરદારો હતા. ગીરિયામાનાં સ્ત્રી નેતા મે કટી લીલી, નાંદીના કોઈટાલેલ, માસાઈના મૂબાટેયાની, કિકુયુના વાયાકી, આરબ કેન્યાવા સીઓના મઝરુઈ કીસીના સ્ત્રી નેતા બોનારીરી, વકામ્બાના ઇટુમામુકા, ટાઈટાના મ્વાંગેકા અને માઉ માઉના કીમાથી ...

આવું જ ઐતિહાસિક સરખાપણું જોઈ ઘણાં દેશ પ્રેમી એશિયન કેન્યાવાસીઓએ આ દેશની આઝાદીની લડતમાં દિલોજાનથી ભાગ લીધેલ.

સૌજન્ય : "અલક મલક", ઓગસ્ટ ૧૯૮૬; પૃ. ૧૨-૧૩.

Nazmi Durrani: Historical Review of South Asian Presence in Kenya

Introduction

The phenomenon of a large number of Asians accepting Kenya as their homeland will soon complete a hundred years. So it is appropriate to review our history at this juncture. Why did our forefathers leave their motherland and migrate in search of a new homeland?

The link between East Africa and India has been there for thousands of years. These were commercial relations. Trade between Africa and Asia was carried out through the Indian Ocean for centuries. As a result of this, a few Indians had settled in the coastal areas of this continent. Similarly, some Africans had also settled in different parts of India. Their descendants, known as Sidi, are found even today.

This long relationship was forcibly cut off by the Portuguese imperialists in the 16th century. With this, the resources and wealth of these two continents were carried to Europe. At the end of the 17th century the Portuguese imperialists were defeated in an armed struggle and lost their control over the Indian Ocean. As a result, relationships between East Africa, Arabia and western India were resumed. The traders and sailors coming from India were mainly from Gujarat province.

But this link did not last long because a new aggressor entered the region. This time the destroyers of the link were the British imperialists. Initially they captured the western part of India and later slowly brought the whole country under their rule. Many brave people resisted them and were martyred.

Under the pretext of ending slave trade, British imperialists started attacking East Africa in the 19th century and by the end of the century, established their rule. At this time, many parts of the world were under the British Empire.

The settlement of Indians in East Africa during the 19th century was only a part of the settlements elsewhere in the British Empire. For example, after 1834 many Indians were taken to the British colonies in West Indies such as Jamaica, Trinidad, Guyana, among others, to work on sugar plantations. Apart from this, workers were taken to South Africa, Mauritius, Fiji and many other countries.

Apparently these workers were taken to the foreign lands after they had voluntarily signed an agreement. But there were two kinds of pressure on them: those who went looking for jobs in cities were made to sign either forcibly or deceitfully by the British companies. On the other hand, most of these people were so poor that they had no choice but to migrate to foreign lands for livelihood. We will discuss the causes of such a miserable condition later in this article.

There was not that much difference between the condition of the workers brought on contract from the other British colonies and the African slaves taken forcibly during the 15th and 19th centuries. The fate of these workers was in the hands of their British employers. They were made to work for 20 hours a day, were beaten with whips, were not allowed freedom of movement even during their free time, were not paid for six months, and so on. They had no right to complain against such ill-treatment.

In East Africa, Indian workers were made to sign such an agreement and were brought to work on the railway tracks being constructed between Kenya and Uganda. Between 1896 and 1903 about 32,000 workers came to Kenya. Out of these 2,500 died as a result of accidents or illness, 6,500 were sent home because they were injured, 16,000 left when the period of their contract was over or the project was completed, and 6,700 decided to settle in East Africa.

Prior to this, a few traders and their employees had already settled in Kenya. These firms were located in coastal villages but they visited the interior regions of East Africa for business purposes. Their businesses expanded during the last decade of the century. As a result, some more people from India came to Kenya. At the same time people whose financial condition was not so good saved some money and came from Porbandar, Karachi or Mumbai ports to East Africa by sea in search of work.

The above description raises a question regarding the economic condition of India, that is today's India, Pakistan and Bangladesh, in the 19th century. Why did millions of people leave their country and travel thousands of miles to settle in alien parts of the world? During the process many people got killed and many more suffered before they were accepted in foreign lands. Was their condition in the motherland worse than all this suffering and death?

To find the answer to this question we need to know the history of India under the British rule.

A Brief History of India Under British rule

The question is, what economic conditions in India during the British rule forced thousands of Indians to migrate from their motherland and settle in alien countries in various parts of the world?

From 1757 to 1857 the British ruled India through the East India Company (The Company Government). In 1857 there was a revolt in an attempt to overthrow the foreign rule. The revolt continued for two years and it was suppressed. Thereafter the British government took over the reign which continued until 1947. During this period the British created divisions among Indians to break their unity. Particularly, Hindus and Muslims were kept divided. From the 1857 revolt, the British had learnt a lesson that if these two communities fight together, British rule in India would soon come to an end. For example, the leaders of the revolution included Mangal Pandey, Ahmed Shah, Laxmibai (The Queen of Jhansi), Bahadurshah Zafar (Mughal Emperor), and Tatya

Tope.

We find many such examples of Hindu–Muslim unity. At the beginning of the 20th century when the British decided to divide Bengal on the basis of religion, both Hindu and Muslims fought against the plan jointly. Under the leadership of Rabindranath Tagor, Abdul Rasul Surendranath Banerji and others, the people of Bengal started a nationalist movement. They raised the slogan of Vande Mataram [Long live the Motherland] and boycotted British goods. This protest compelled the imperialists to give up their plan.

A similar example is found in the second decade of the twentieth century in Punjab. At that time a countrywide movement against exploitation and oppression was going on under the leadership of Dr. Keechlu and Dr. Satyapal. In 1919, the Hindus, Sikhs and Muslims of Punjab organised marches and went on strikes. Their slogan was 'Victory to Hindu–Muslim'. The government was scared, so their army attacked unarmed people at Jallianwala Baug killing over a thousand of them and injuring many more.

There are many such instances of unity among the people of different communities in the fight for India's freedom. The British rulers tried hard to break this unity and create divisions on religious grounds. But finally they succeeded and in 1947, India was partitioned.

During the 200 years of British rule in India, one thing was constant and that is exploitation and plundering of resources. The British attacked India, defeated their opponents and captured the country. The irony is that they made the Indians pay the amount they had spent on this operation. During the first 30 years of the 19th century, the imperialists made them pay 700 million pounds. Every year India had to pay a certain amount of money to the British government. If they failed to make this payment for some reason they had to pay with compound interest at the rate of 12%. For example, in the year 1901 -1902, the amount of interest to be paid was seventeen million pounds.

Centuries before British rule in India, Indian artefacts were known all over the world. The British destroyed Indian handicrafts in order to promote their factory goods. They compelled the artisans and craftsmen to pay taxes to the imperialist government. They were ordered to sell their goods only through the government agent, and that too at very low prices. If the order was not followed, workshops were set on fire, the hands of craftsmen were cut off or they were killed outright. As a result of this cruel policy, thousands of people lost their lives or occupations.

The condition of farmers was no better. The government had levied a very high tax (lagaan) on agricultural land. Irrespective of whether the crop was good or bad, the farmer had to pay the tax. Previously if the crop was good, the farmer used to set some of it aside for the future when the crop might fail. But now because of the tax, the farmers were struggling even when the crop was good. If the farmers failed to pay the tax their farms would be auctioned. The farmers had to borrow money on interest to pay the tax, and if it was not repaid on time, the money lenders would confiscate their land. This made thousands of farmers landless.

Many people became victims of hunger. During the first half of the 19th century there were seven droughts in various parts of the country, killing 500,000 people. As compared to this in the latter half of the same century, there were droughts and 20,000,000 people died of starvation.

The landless farmers left their villages and moved to cities in search of jobs. But the foreign rulers had destroyed the native industries so there were no jobs. Under these difficult circumstances it was natural for people to migrate to foreign lands for survival and better life. This led them to the other parts of the British Empire.

Part 3

By the end of the 18th century, the British had lost their empire in North America. Along with this, they also lost their control over land holdings. But in the first half of the 19th century, they had victory over the French so they captured the islands previously controlled by France and started large scale cultivation of cash crops (e.g. sugarcane). There was a shortage of workers in these regions, so contracted (bonded) workers were taken from India. At the end of this century, when they strengthened their reign in South and East Africa, they brought the Indian workers here too.

The Indians who came to East Africa were of two categories: bonded labourers who were brought to construct the railways, and traders and their employees. As the British reign became stronger, so did their administration also increase. The British settlers had taken away fertile agricultural land from its African owners. Villages and cities expanded. So more workers were needed. Craftsmen like joiners, engineers, blacksmiths, masons, painters, tailors, cobblers, among others, came from India. The government also needed clerks and accountants for their offices and banks. Many English–speaking Indians were also encouraged to come. In addition, some teachers, lawyers and doctors were also brought. Moreover, the children of these Indian settlers were encouraged to receive such professional education.

However, the British government particularly encouraged traders. The imperialists wanted the Indian traders to set up businesses in every part of the country. They had a two-fold benefit from this. One, the African people would spend more money to buy commodities. They would need cash so they would have to work on the British settlers' farms. Two, the shopkeepers would sell the goods produced by British firms. Such goods were imported from Britain to East Africa through British steamers, the cargo was insured with the British insurance companies, while the earnings of the traders were deposited in British banks. So ultimately, profits would go to British capitalists, but the risk of running businesses in foreign land was borne by the Indian traders.

Thus in East Africa and their colonies in other parts of the world, the British rulers used Indian settlers for the exploitation of native people. Apart from this, the people in the British colonies were exploited and oppressed in many other ways. For example, in India, the British rulers ruined peasant farmers by forcibly collecting Lagaan (tax on land) from them. Similarly, in Kenya a tax was levied on every household which was known as 'Hut Tax'. During the last decade of the previous century, the British settlers snatched away thousands of cows and goats from the Kenyan herdsmen. They took possession of thousands of acres of fertile land and turned the regional land owners into labourers.

One finds much similarity between the conditions in Kenya and India during the foreign rule. This is not only in the manner of exploitation and oppression by the British imperialists but also in the revolt of the native peoples against it.

In India fighters like Tatya Tope, Laxmibai, the Queen of Jhansi, Khudiram Bose, Ashfaq Ullah Khan, Chandra Shekhar Azad, Bhagat Singh, Subhash Chandra Bose and his colleagues Shahnawaz Khan and Laxmibai Swaminathan and many others took up arms against the foreign invaders. Similarly, in Kenya, many patriots fought the British with arms. The leaders of armed struggle included: female leader of Giriama Me Katilili, Koitalel of Nandi, Mbatiyan of Masai, Waiyaki of Kikuyu, Mazrui of Arab Kenyans, female leader Bonariri of Kisina, Itumamuka of Wakamba, Mwangeka of Taita and Kimaathi of Kikuyu's Mau Mau struggle.

Inspired by this similarity, many patriotic Asian Kenyans participated whole–heartedly in the fight for Kenya's freedom.

Alakmalak June(Part 1), August (Part 2), December (Part 3) 1986.

Nazmi Durrani: Background to Class Formation and Class Struggle

Under British rule, a form of apartheid was practiced in Kenya by the colonial authority which favoured the European settlers. Fertile agricultural land in the highlands was taken over by the British colonial administration for settlement of white farmers who mostly came from Britain or South Africa. The original African owners were rendered landless and homeless, and were forced to provide labour on the now European settler-owned farms. In towns, the best residential areas were set aside for Europeans. Asians could only live in specially designated areas which were generally situated between European areas (with a portion of "no man's land" in between) and those allocated for Africans. The African areas were the poorest, where tens of thousands of people were crowded into small sections with little or no amenities. In health, education, and in fact in every sphere, the three racial groups were provided with highly discriminatory and strictly segregated facilities. Those for the Europeans were by far the best, with those for the Africans being either non-existent or of very poor quality.

In the colonial political field, the Legislative Council and municipal councils were entirely dominated by European settlers and administrators. The Asians were given a nominal representation in these institutions. (In 1917, M. A. Desai was chosen to represent the Asian community in the settler controlled Nairobi Municipal Council). However, the African majority was excluded altogether from these bodies.

A main demand of the Indian Association, which was the organisational arm of the Asian Kenyans trading class, was for representation equal to the European settlers in these councils. It also wanted the representatives to be elected and not nominated by the colonial administration.

In keeping with the two distinct classes of Asian Kenyans who had made the country their home, their anti- British campaign was also of two types. One class of Indian immigrants were petty traders who had started settling on the East Africa coast since the middle of the 19th century. With the colonial conquest of Kenya by the British, who had also conquered India, increasing numbers of traders were encouraged to settle here. This was intended to facilitate the penetration of British manufactured goods into the country. Following the first influx of these traders, many peasants and workers who were rendered landless and jobless during occupation of India migrated to East Africa where they initially worked for the early traders. Later they opened their own little shops in the interior. Some of these were later to become commercial and industrial giants, while the majority remained as retail traders, the so called *dukawallas*.

The second group of Indian immigrants were workers who had been brought into the country to build the railway. During the period 1896-1903, about 32,000 workers were hired. Over a half of this number eventually returned to India on completion of their contracts. Some 2,500 lost their lives on the job. 6,500 had to be sent back because of illness and injury suffered during the construction work, with many of them having suffered lifelong disabilities. About 6,724 settled in Kenya and Uganda on completion of their work. These were skilled and semi-skilled workers who formed the nucleus of the Asian Kenyan working class in the early years of the century. They were employed in the railway workshops and in the government public works department around the country, with others setting up their own independent little workshops in towns. Later, some of them were employed in the emergent private industrial sector. Their numbers were augmented by the coming of skilled workers (masons, plumbers, blacksmiths, carpenters) who found employment in the construction industry, and others such as shoemakers, tailors, and mechanics to service the growing populations of urban centres. Along with these wage-earning workers, there were salaried workers who were employed at clerical levels in the colonial administration and commercial sector, and professions such as teachers and accountants.

The petty bourgeois and working classes led two distinct struggles. The former fought for equal opportunities with the European settlers in the economic and political spheres. The later organised themselves, along with their African workers, into trade unions and fought for just returns for their labour. The first recorded organised resistance against colonial employers took place almost with the very introduction of workers in the country, namely the 1900 railway workers' strike. The working class struggle was, by the late 1940's, to develop into a formidable political instrument against the British colonial system as a whole. The colonial response to the workers' struggle was much more severe than that to the constitutional struggle against institutional racial discrimination. The colonial authorities resorted to jailing and deportation of its leaders right from the earliest days. For example, following the 1914 strike of the railway and public works department workers, their leaders Mehrchard Puri and Tirath Ram were arrested and forcibly deported from the country.

Nazmi Durrani: Kenya's Fight for Freedom, An Introductory Reader

FREEDOM FIGHTERS

Baserion (Nandi)

Bonariri (Gusii)

Ebei (Turkana)

Fumo Bakari (Swahili)

Gero (Luo)

Itumo Muka (Kamba)

Koitalel arap Samoei (Nandi

Lowalel (Turkana)

Mohammad Abdille (Somali)

Mbaruk bin Rashid (Arab Kenyan)

Mbatiani (Maasai)

Mi Katilili (Giriama)

Moraa (Gusii)

Mutero (Embu)

Mwangeka (Taita)

Njama (Embu)

Nyagudi wuod Ogambe (Seme, Luo)

Sendeu (Maasai)

Wanje Mwadorikola (Giriama)

Waiyaki wa Hinga (Kikuyu)

When the British first invaded Kenya, the Kenyan people fought back. They fought for their freedom. In the following pages, we see some examples of this fight by people from different parts of the country.

INTRODUCTION

One hundred years ago, Europeans from a country called England or Britain came to Kenya.

These British people forcefully took away cows, goats and sheep from our people.

They forced people to pay money (taxes) to them.

Their army killed our people. Women and men, children and old people were killed. Or people's houses and villages were burnt.

They forcefully took away land from the people of our country. They gave this land to European farmers. They forced people to work on these farms.

The European owners of the farms got a lot of money. The Kenyan workers on these farms got very little money.

The people became very poor. The children did not have enough food.

The people knew that they must get their land back.

They knew that they must be free; they must make their country free.

They knew they had to fight.

People from all over Kenya fought. They fought bravely. They fought without fear.

From beginning when the British tried to conquer the country, when they tried to make Kenya a colony, the people fought back.

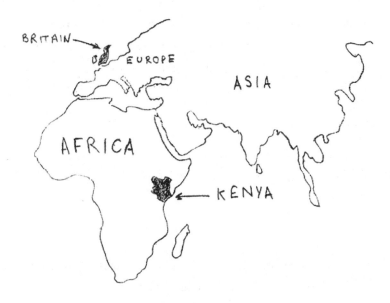

Here some examples of people's resistance to colonialism.

Bukusu

The British army tried to conquer the land belonging to the people. The Bukusu fought fiercely against the invaders.

In 1895, they fought two famous battles against the British: at Lumboka Fort and at Chetambe Fort.

EMBU

The British wanted to conquer the land of the Embu people because of the rich forests in this area.

Before 1904 they tried six times to get a foothold in this part of the country. They were defeated all six times by the Embu warriors.

Their leaders were NJAMA and MATERO.

GIRIAMA

The British wanted to steal the farming land belonging to the Giriama.

They wanted the young people to leave their homes and work on European plantations. They also wanted the young Giriama to work as porters to carry goods for the British army. They tried to force the Giriama to pay taxes to the British government.

The Giriama refused. They fought a war against the British army in 1914.

Their leader was MANYZI WA MENZA, a woman. She was known as MI KATILILI. She was helped by another leader, a man known as WANJE MWADORIKOLA.

GUSII

In the land of the Gusii people, the British army captured thousands upon thousands of livestock. They also burnt people's houses.

From 1905 onwards the Gusii fought many fierce battles.

One of their brave leaders was MORAA, a woman. She encouraged the people to fight without fear.

Moraa was shot and captured in one of the battles against the British army.

In 1920 another woman leader, BONARIRI of Kitutu led the Gusii against the British.

KAMBA

The Kamba people opposed the British intruders when they tried to conquer their country in 1899.

The Kamba warriors fought fiercely against British askaris near the Kangundo Hills.

Their leader was ITUMO MUKA.

KIKUYU

The British stole food crops from the Kikuyu people. They took away cows, goats and sheep by force. They burnt people's houses.

The Kikuyu defended themselves bravely against these invaders and defeated them. The British army was forced to build many forts to protect themselves from the Kikuyu warriors.

The Kikuyu leader was WAIYAKI WA HINGA. He was murdered by the British in 1892.

The Kikuyu carried on fighting. Many battles were fought and won by their soldiers. Their leader at the time was NGUNJU WA GAKERE.

KIPSIGIS

The British wanted to steal land belonging to the Kipsigis people. They wanted to give it to European settlers.

The Kipsigis refused to allow them to take away their land. They fought against the British army. They joined with their neighbours, the Nandi, to oppose the British.

The Kipsigis led many attacks against the British fortified post called Fort Ternan.

LUO

THE Luo fought many battles against the British army between 1896 and 1900. The British looted thousands of cows, goats and sheep from the people.

The Kisumu fisher people attacked the British because the British stole their fish.

The Luo of Ugenya-Kager fought fiercely against the British army. Their leader was GERO.

The British stole the Seme people's cattle and food grains. The Seme are part of the Luo people. They fought against the British. They fought many battles.

Their leader was NYAGUDI WUOD OGAMBE.

MAASAI

For a long time, the Maasai kept out the British from their country. Some armed traders, explorers and missionaries tried to forcefully enter this area. They were killed or driven away by Maasai soldiers.

Sometimes trading caravans asked for permission to pass through the Maasai land. They were allowed to pass. But they had to pay taxes to the people.

Before 1890 the leader of the Maasai was MBATIANI.

Afterwards the British took away forcefully the fertile land of the Maasai in Laikipia. They gave this land to European farmers. The Maasai opposed this strongly. Their leader was SENDEU, a son of Mbatiani.

MARAKWET

The Marakwet people of the Rift Valley were well-known for their iron weapons. Their weapons were made by many blacksmiths.

These weapons were used by more than 3,000 soldiers to fight against the British army in 1911-1912.

SWAHILI and ARAB KENYANS

The British tried to conquer Takaungu at the coast. The Swahili and Arab Kenyans fought against the British army.

In 1896 they defeated the British in battles fought at Freretown and Malindi.

These brave warriors were led by MBARUK BIN RASHID of the Mazrui family.

The Swahili people of Witu fought against European invaders. They were first attacked by the British. The British wanted to capture the rich forest land belonging to the Witu people.

The people fearlessly attacked both invading armies. They were led by FUMO BAKARI.

TAITA

The British tried to force the Taita to work as porters to carry goods for their army. They refused.

The British army attacked the Mwanda who are part of the Taita people. A fierce battle was fought in 1892. Many soldiers of the British were killed and injured.

The Taita leader was called MWANGEKA.

TURKANA

The British army tried to conquer the land of the Turkana. The Turkana warriors fought many battles to drive out the British invaders.

One famous battle was fought at Kangalila near Lokitaung on 27 May 1918. The Turkana defeated a British army of more than 1,500 soldiers.

The Turkana were led by LOWALEL and EBEI.

Benegal Pereira: Life and Times of Eddie H. Pereira (1915 – 1995) Indian Nationalist Extraordinaire in Kenya

Eddie H. Pereira - Kisumu, Kenya - September 9, 1946 (Nehru Eddie)[8]

Introduction

In the mid 1940s, the struggle for independence in India fanned the flames of nationalism in Africa. In Kenya, patriotic fervour brought an end to the Colonial governance duplicating the historic events on the Indian sub-continent thus taking a lead in Africa's struggle for independence. Most observers agree that South Asians of Kenya were catalysts in the rise of national self-determination in Africa. Eddie Pereira, based in Kisumu, western Kenya held no political office, and his political convictions and grassroots activities remained largely unrecorded. During the period between 1942 to 1952, this extraordinary young Goan displayed much of his vigour and persistently fought against imperial rule. He demonstrated his patriotic passions and was one of the few Indians who

8. Vita Books would like to thank Benegal Pereira for making these photos and illustrations available for this book.

could be counted on to fight British oppression in those earlier years. He wrote regularly to the press against imperialist rule, as he struggled against British rule both in Kenya and India, and simultaneously against Portuguese control in Goa, his ancestral homeland. Characteristic of his Indian pride, he dressed in full 'khadi', symbolic of his nationalist stance and commitment to the Gandhi movement for Indian independence.

Eddie Pereira, A Bio-sketch

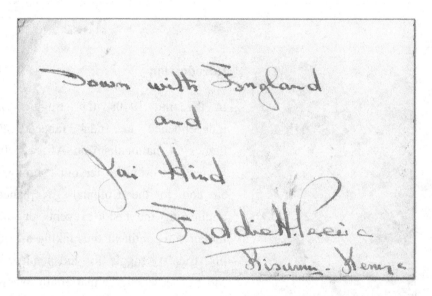

Jai Hind - Written by Eddie . H Pereira - Kisumu Kenya (1946)

On the night before he died, Eddie Pereira wrote a farewell note: "A good character is the best tombstone. Those who loved you and were helped by you, remember you when forget-me-nots are withered". He added: "Carve Your Name On Hearts, Not On Marble" a metaphor that reflects his own legacy. Eddie hand-wrote this touching testimonial, his final words of wisdom composed on the night of January 25, 1995. That was the night his life ended in Nairobi. He was murdered, a crime which remains unsolved.

Eddie was an extraordinary Goan born during the First World War in

Mombasa, Kenya on October 15, 1915. He lived through a still greater war, and more significantly, witnessed the end of colonialism in both India and Kenya and the rise of these new nations from their more or less bloody births and their memories of ancient splendours. Eddie was a passionate Indian nationalist during the colonial period in Kenya, an extraordinary person with unwavering convictions who lived in a tumultuous era wrought with the often-devastating consequences of world wars, fledging steps towards independence of new nations and years of vicious terrorism. Above all, he was a passionate, politically driven man who for six decades made his mark on true "Indian" identity as well as the fierce nationalism of newborn Kenya. The oppressive British Raj in India did not endear itself to the young man bursting with pride in his ancestors, belief in his own self-worth and a vision of liberty in the future of his two countries. In his unpublished autobiography he wrote of these twin passions, which consumed his youthful years:

Mahatma Gandhi and Nehru became my ideals. Now I was looking for higher values of life and sanctity, and in doing so, I was ridiculed and misunderstood. I suffered and was made to suffer. I was even imprisoned because I dared to speak the truth. No nation can continue half slave and half free. In India, the Congress High Command decided that the time was ripe for revolution, and that the Congress Party or any Indian Party for the matter of it should resort to non-violent struggle for liberation. I for one was for armed struggle. In India, the resolution was officially labeled "QUIT INDIA". I ventured in Kenya into newspaper articles, on emancipation; nothing was ever over to be anti-anything that was non-Indian as far as I was concerned, at the myth of an innate European superiority, and the Indian running dogs, unless I ran out of ink and paper.

Though born in Kenya, Eddie early traveled back to his ancestral homeland, India, to extend his formal education. He attended schools in the state of Karnataka, originally known as Mysore, attending St. Paul's, a Jesuit school in

Belgaum, St Pancreas High School in the southern city of Bellary, and later, St. Xavier's College, where he graduated with honorary degrees in literature and practical politics. He became a four-anna Congress Member, embracing the ideals of a prejudice-free society. The Pereiras belonged to the ancient Chardo clan of the Kshatriya caste of Goa. Eddie's pride in his warrior ancestry is well documented in his autobiography:

> If records are to be trusted, the Chardo Kshatriya lineage had its origin in the annals of the epic narratives of the Ramayana. Our ancestors derived their inspiration from the heroes of Raghuvamsha ... We all call ourselves Chalukya Chardo Kshatriyas and so we belong to a warrior caste of the fourfold social order in ancient India ... Shri Ramachandra, King of Ajodhya, is the hero of the Ramayana, one of the sacred epics of India. . .This Ayodhya of Ramchandra was the Chardo place of origin. Chardos are mainly found in Goa and the surrounding area out of Goa. Chardo Kshatriyas originate from the high ideals of unity and freedom, they have in them the spirit of bravery of their indomitable ancestors. They never held their personal life dear, and welcomed even death in the later years of their struggle. Yet they had to migrate from place to place to keep their tradition culture and the way of life intact.

By the time Eddie returned to Kenya in the late 1930s, there was little doubt that he was a radical espousing valiant solutions to national problems. His reasoning was clear. His agenda was pragmatic. Based in western Kenya in the Kisumu township, Eddie centred his campaign at the local thoroughfare of the town centre's clock tower, frequently waving the Indian flag with calls of "Jai Hind", a maxim synonymous with the 'Quit India' movement. Symbolic of his pride in Indian nationalism, Eddie Pereira wore 'khadi' symbolic of his commitment to the Gandhi movement for Indian independence. He was opposed to the authoritative British rule in India as well as the Portuguese dominance in Goa. These twin conflicts bolstered his fierce opposition to the imperial British regime in Kenya. His convictions about the ill effects of colonialism ran so deep that one gets the impression that he wanted to take on imperialism with his bare hands:

Frankly I felt very free. Ventured into the African continent in Kenya more stranded than making my way, remained unrecorded for the present, but the argument of my whole life as it had been lived is a state of completeness in a struggle of a civilisation with a hostile environment, in which the destiny of British and Portuguese rule became necessarily involved. I do not think that any apologies are expected from me for a good deal of egoistic matter. . .. They say, a scoundrel's last resort is politics; if that is so, that is what really happen to me! Whatever it was, I took up politics (Indian Freedom fighting) very seriously and became very unpopular with the Goan community who were pro Portuguese and English at the time.

The nationalist and freedom-loving Eddie Pereira was an ardent supporter of Kenya's Mau Mau rebellion. He was deported from the Nandi Hill tea farming area by the British administration for his anti-Colonial activities. Between 1948 and 1952, Eddie worked in a Saw Mill in the dense Elburgon Forest. When Mau Mau activities arose in the region, Eddie lent his support to their cause and was recognised and respected by many fighters in the forest. Owing to his anti-British activities, he was asked to leave the Forest concession and dismissed from the Elburgon Forest Mills by order of the European Forest Officer, under suspicion of giving land to detainee's wives to cultivate. After leaving the Elburgon Saw Mills he joined the Cooper Motor Corporation in Nakuru. He covertly visited Elburgon Forest again where he was detained for transporting freedom fighters from Elburgon to Nakuru and was charged and heavily fined. As a result, he was fired from Copper Motor Corporation.

The Mau Mau quest for Kenyan independence justified their methodologies for Eddie. Indeed, in the years that followed, he became a constant thorn in the sides of the British and Portuguese hegemony. He was imprisoned for his overt anti-British views and actions. His staunch anti-colonial stance would eventually result in his deportation from several provinces of British Kenya. His characteristic full tilt manner frequently clashed with pro-Portuguese Goan loyalists and there were strong indications that the Portuguese would bar him from ever returning to Goa. The "loyalists" in Goa who preferred to emulate the Portuguese elicited sharp criticism from Eddie who saw in them fellow Indians who had turned their backs on their own traditions:

> They detested and hated to be called Indians but rather Goans. They tried their very best to emulate the good qualities of the Portuguese, but stayed with the bad one. At times they were more Portuguese than the Portuguese themselves, and ended in being cedar vanished Portuguese, without any identity, in other words, just sons of bitches. Outwardly, they looked Indian. With that, all resemblance between them and us ended. They represented an extreme of deracination, of vacuity, which still fascinates me. The act of conversion had left them culturally shipwrecked.

Eddie's continued opposition to British imperialism in Kenya, the inflammatory anti-British articles he wrote for Kenyan newspapers resulted in Eddie's imprisonment by the Kenyan authorities in 1957. The Nakuru Police's charge (the colonial Kenyan government) was that Eddie had exchanged his broken down radio for a new radio while it was still under hire-purchase terms. Eddie knew that the charge was a cooked-up one but in his panic he pleaded guilty which resulted in his imprisonment. Eddie's fortitude while in prison reveals the many aspects of his personality - his sensitive nature, his fierce pride and his belief in the moral superiority of his cause. Eddie called the prison, "the symbolic centre of modern society," and wrote about his experiences in that solitary community in great detail in his autobiography:

> I was sentenced and imprisoned in 1957 February for six months. Heaven's ominous silence over all. Bureaucratised world to me from

my inner spiritual life became an obsessive object of contemplation, madman and saint, clown and saviour, confined in what might be called the symbolic centre of modern society: the prison. I was simply appalled, to be perfectly frank, it smacked of a vendetta, or jealousy, or politics, I groaned a dastardly attempt to discredit me. The stabs shall heal no more; I will never forgive the English, I scorn them. For no reason other than being anti British, anti-imperialism, anti-White settlers, supporting Mau Mau and fighting for Kenya's freedom and against apartheid in Kenya.

In his defence, Eddie maintained that "having paid over three-quarter of the price is not subject under hire purchase terms and that I was free to trade it." The appeal, lodged immediately by counsel J.M. Nazareth Q.C. was deliberately delayed, but was eventually upheld and Eddie was released after 105 days in prison without apology or compensation. Eddie sardonically called it "the British justice." At the time of his arrest, Eddie held a number of key positions with nationalist, anti-imperialist organisations. He knew that the British would arrest him on any charge, credible or not. He was Secretary General of the Indian Association, Nakuru; on the executive council of the E.A. Indian National Congress, Nairobi, under the leadership of Shivabhai Amin (1956); on the board of the E.A. Goan Congress; President of the Goan Institute, Nakuru, President of the Goan Union, Nakuru, and Chairman of the Goan Education Council. Eddie writes in his autobiography that he was mistaken "for a Communist when he might have been a fellow traveler and a friend of convenience, I was declared Nationalist and extreme left Socialist":

I had written over 100 articles in the press against British and colonial rule in Kenya, and had coughed out fines several times for writing sedition. My political agitation against the British started from 1940 and openly I donned Khadi. Some rare special treatment was extended to me by the request of the Special Branch of the Police who visited me almost daily for a friendly chat, they were seeking information of the workings of the Indian Association and the E.A. Congress, they also had a guilty complex for putting me in prison for no crime at all and this was proved when my appeal was upheld. The British ideals and objectives of yesterday were still the ideals of today, but they had lost some of their lustre and, even as one seems to go towards them, they lost the shining beauty, which had warmed the heart and vitalised the body. Evil triumphed often enough but what was far worse was the coarsening and distortion of what seemed so right. Was British nature so essentially bad that it would take ages of training, through suffering and misfortune, before it could behave reasonably and rise man above that creature of lust and violence and deceit that they now are?

Prison life was an "unrelieved horror" to Eddie who was often described as a man of gregarious and sybaritic nature. In those days, African jails were little more than mere "torture houses, producing crime and lunacy in equal measure."

My first days were spent where I could scarcely breathe in the fetid air of my cell and was at first, quite unable to eat the food which was insufficient and inedible, which always produced diarrhoea, the mere sight and smell of which made me vomit. When hunger at last forced me to eat, I suffered from diarrhoea and became so weak that I could hardly stand. In spite of exhaustion I could not sleep on my plank bed, and at nights I suffered from the wildest delusions. The filthy unsanitary conditions in which the prisoners lived, and the punishment of insomnia inflicted on all. I had not yet learnt how to speak to the other convicts during my daily exercise without moving my lips, and one day I heard a man behind me say: "I am sorry for you; it is harder for the likes of you than it is for the likes of us", I replied, "No, we all suffer alike." I was spared none of the cruelties and indignities which unimaginative human being wreak upon those who fall into their power; and as one who belonged to a different social class from the other African prisoners, I was the special victim of that pettiness and spite which the majority of those who have been subjected to authority display whenever they have a chance to exercise it.

Eddie had resolved to stamp out the imperial arrogance of the time. As the years went by, his convictions did not change, but he was seen more as a visionary when India and Kenya gained their independence, Eddie became less politically active but he never abandoned his rebellious pursuits. His rejection of tyranny remained strong. His passionate love for India and Kenya endured to the end of his life.

In 1969 Eddie opened and what became a well-known restaurant and inn which he had named, Chateau Pereira. The restaurant was located in the town of Kisumu, in Western Kenya where Eddie ran it with his three sons. The restaurant became a successful landmark and in its seven years of existence, the remarkable tales and stories of its many patrons speak volumes. Patron Fatima Jappie-Fadaka wrote, "Eddie roars like a lion, swears like a sailor and holds his own very original views. However, after getting to know him, one realizes that he can bleat like a lamb, converse like a master and shake most people out of the complacency of their own long-held views and beliefs. He says exactly what he thinks and damn the consequence, but never with malice. In a by-gone age he would probably have been burnt at the stake. Thank goodness he has escaped that fate, as the world would be a poorer place without him. With people like Eddie, there is hope yet. Carry on the good work."

Although born a Christian, Eddie, reverted to his Hindu roots in 1976. He took a Vedic name, Sadashiva and practiced the virtues of his Hindu beliefs until his untimely death. He requested that upon his death he be cremated in the Hindu tradition. Portions of Eddie's ashes were scattered across four continents, largely in the rivers of the wilderness of Kenya. A portion of his ashes were returned to his ancestral home and immersed in the waters of the Mandovi River in Tivim, Goa. Other portions of his remains were placed at the graves of his mother in Sidcup, England and that of his eldest son, in Manchester, New Hampshire, USA.

Kenya and India lost a true son in Eddie Pereira. His unsolved murder in Nairobi on January 25, 1995 left an immeasurable void. Thankfully, he made an unforgettable impression on everyone who knew him for what he was. Eddie was a man who fought all forms of injustice relentlessly. He inspired others with a never-ending passion for both individual and collective freedoms, and for what he believed to be the truth. Eddie will be remembered for his consistent commitment to lofty, yet practical principles, his nobility of mind and the radiant warmth of his deep feelings for his fellow men. Perhaps most of all, Eddie will be remembered for his colourful personality. Kind and unselfish to a fault, he gave most of his worldly possessions to those in need.

At the time of death, Eddie left behind the manuscripts of three books. One was to be his autobiography, while the others two were entitled, *A Trail Blazer Century: The History of Indians in Kenya and Goans in Kenya: A New Breed.* Unfinished, they are awaiting publication.

GOAN DIVISIONS IN EAST AFRICA

Much of the 'divided and rule' bluster propagated by the imperialistic governance can initially be drawn from the official census polls that counted Goans as a separate race, from other Indian communities that were all grouped together. All South Asians living in Kenya at the time hailed from the Indian subcontinent. Pereira et all say, "The Goan community in Kenya, about 8000 strong at its peak in the mid 1960s and before Kenya's independence, represented at best just about 3 percent of the total 280,000 persons". [9]

During the period leading up to India's independence on August 15, 1947, the

9. See: Pereira, Benegal, et al. (2013): Fragments of a Legacy' . Awaaz Magazine, May/ June.

division between the Goan community and the wider Indian sects of Kenya came to ahead. The question of whether Goans in Kenya should preserve their Portuguese identities or throw in their lot with the wider Indian communities came into focus. The convening of the East African Goan Conference in Mombasa in December of 1946, initiated much of this discussion.10 The dilemma on whether Goans should mix themselves with the other Indian sects presented itself to the East African Indian National Congress (EAINC) in 1945. A. B. Patel and the so-called Mombasa group refused to accept the presidency of Dr. A.C.L. De Souza, who was a prominent Kenya Legislative Council member. Instead, J.M. Nazareth became president of EAINC, but resigned in 1952 and setup a bona fide East African Goan National Association (EAGNA). Much of these rifts within the South Asian community could easily be seen as a consequence of the division and advantage between the sects in the colony.

The debate on the whether Goans would count themselves as Indians caused a rage in the Indian press between the factions. A more recent assertion of this position is articulated by Fernandes (2016) who says "despite the injustices against the Africans, many Goans thought well of the British. Goans must be the only race of its kind to have loved its colonial oppressors and thought of them close to God. Unlike other South Asians, Goans had made no substantial bid for freedom from Goa's colonial masters, the Portuguese, in the twentieth century. There were a group of freedom fighters in Goa who did their best" 11 In Kenya, Eddie H. Pereira of Kisumu was one of a few passionate Goans to make his mark and take on imperialism head on, as reflected in these letters to the Colonial Times Newspaper in East Africa.

——

10. *The Goan Voice* Nairobi. 1949 – 1950.
11. Fernandes, Cyprian(2016): *Yesterday in Paradise*. Bloomington, IN, USA: Balboa Press.
   http://bookstore.balboapress.com/Products/SKU-001078410/Yesterday-in-Paradise.aspx
   [Accessed: 09-10-16].

About the Author

Benegal Pereira was born in Kenya and grew up there during the turbulent times of the Mau Mau uprising. He saw the end of colonial rule in Kenya and migrated to England in 1978, and later to the United states in 1986. He currently resides in Amherst in the State of New Hampshire, USA. Witnessing his father's dedication to the cause of freedom for Kenya and the Indian sub-continent, Benegal has vivid memories of the tensions and rancorous divisions associated with the movement of the East African countries toward self-determination. In 1998, Benegal founded the East African forum, 'Namaskar-Africana' which has since attracted the participation of former East African Asians from all quarters of the globe. Benegal's avocation is the collection of postcolonial printed material on East Africa, a passion sustained by his love for his birthplace and what he believes is a largely untold story of the South Asian contribution to East Africa's flourishing freedom. He possesses one of the world's largest private collections of printed materials devoted solely to this subject.

A Selection of Eddie Pereira's letters to Kenyan press

"I had written over 100 articles in the press against British and colonial rule in Kenya, and had coughed out fines several times for writing sedition" - Eddie Pereira. The following are a small selection of his Letters to local press.

Letter to The COLONIAL TIMES

"Africa's largest selling Indian weekly"

"These Whites"

The Editor, *Colonial Times*

Sir - Once again the Settler Press has started agitating and they are going to have it. In the column of the *Kenya Weekly News* in the issue of 31st August an ugly article appeared under the heading "THESE INDIANS". The heading alone is sufficient to curdle our blood. I am sure many of us have read the article, if not, it is advisable to

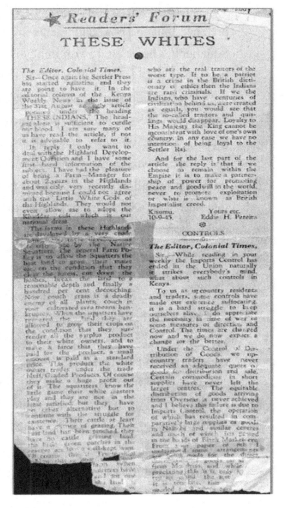

refer to it.

In reply, I only want to deal with the Highland Development Question and I have some first hand information on the subject. I have had the pleasure of being a Farm Manager for about two years in the Highlands and was only very recently dismissed because I could not agree with the Little White Gods of the Highlands. They would not even allow me to adopt the Khaddar cult which is our national dress.

The farms in these Highlands are developed by a very crude pretence, but these developments are only done by the Native Squatters. The general Farm Policy is to allow the Squatters the best land to grow their maize, etc, on the condition that they clear the forest, cut down the bushes, break the land to a reasonable depth and finally a hundred percent de-couching. Now couch grass is a deadly enemy of all plants; couch in your cultivated area means bankruptcy. When the squatters have prepared the land they are allowed to grow their crops on the condition that they surrender all the surplus product to their white owners, and to make a farce that they have paid as a standard price. This product the white owner trades under the trade bluff, Graded Products. Of course they make a huge profit out of it. The squatters know the little game their white masters play and are not in the least satisfied, but they have no other alternative but to continue the struggle for existence. The cattle at least have a chance of grazing, the little green patches in the reserve are like well-kept lawn. Of course this is Trusteeship... and this how the native squatter is exploited...... who are the real traitors of the worst type ? If to be a patriot is a crime in the British dictionary of ethics then Indian are rank criminals. If the Indians, who have centuries of civilization behind us, were created as equals, you would see that the so called traitors and quislings would disappear. Loyalty to His Majesty the King cannot be inconsistent with love of one's own country. In any case we have no intention of being loyal to the Settler Raj.

And for the last part of the article the reply is that if we choose to remain within the Empire it is to make partnership for power for promoting peace and goodwill in the world, never to promote exploitation or what is known as British Imperialist creed.

Yours etc.

Eddie H. Pereira

Kisumu,

10-9-45

"The Establishment of Venomous Influence" … Equality for Goans

The Editor, Colonial Times,

Sir, The unchecked race of the Whites of this country [standing] for the establishment of their venomous and dominating influence in the political and economic fields of the country, [...] in the sinister garb of the self-appointed trustees of millions of the dumb "God-children" of this soil has timely alarmed the other vigilant communities.

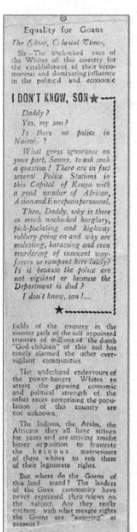

The underhand endeavours of the power hungry Whites to arrest the growing economic and political strength of the other races comprising the population of this country are not unknown.

The Indians, the Arabs, the Africans they have all striven for years, and are striving amidst bitter opposition, to frustrate the heinous manoeuvres of these whites to rob them of their legitimate rights.

But where do the Goans of this land stand? The leaders of the Goan community have never expressed their views on the subject. Are they really content with what meagre rights the Goans are "enjoying" at present?

Is it not high time that the leaders of the Goan community cast away their years old timidity and declare in bold and unequivocal terms the legitimate aspirations of the Goans for equality in all walks of life in the country?

Jai Hind

Your etc.

Eddie H. Pereira

Kisumu,

22-12-45

Goans' Unity

The Editor, Colonial Times,

We Goans in East Africa have aped the West one sided only, that is in fashions, dresses, dances, language, etc, etc but have failed to be Patriots to our Mother Country, which is certainly unlike the European way to life, to live like slaves to eternity. I am unable to see you love your country less than a Nationalist, if it is a question of time, when will you throw in your lot as a community with the reformers who are hungering to free Indians from the curse of White domination. NOW IS THE TIME, remembering that the unity is strength and not merely a copy book maxim.

At the present moment, we Goans have nothing to share with other communities, and ahead of us is wilderness, conflict, struggle, despondency and despair, it is proof that our slavery is complete as we have been hugging these whites and have kept aloof from Indian politics which concern us most. Accept my evidence that the rest of the Indian communities are sick of our aloofness. Therefore, I ask you to choose the better way and make common cause with the other communities. Indian Nationalism is not exclusive, nor aggressive, nor destructive. It is health-giving, religious and therefore humanitarian.

The Goan Nationalist Youth can avert this catastrophe no matter what difficulties be in our path, we must make the clearest possible declaration that we are INDIAN FIRST, MEN FIRST and subjects afterwards.

JAI HIND

Your etc.,

Eddie H. Pereira

Kisumu.

31st January, 1946

GOANS IN EAST AFRICA

To the Editor, *East African Standard*

Sir, -- "Would Goans mix themselves up with the political life of the Indian Community?" The answer is "certainly yes, and as Congressman". We mix because they are our flesh and blood. Congress is our political unit because we have digested the 20 Congress Commandments, which suit us. I would ask my Goan comrades not to be led by disruptions, not to distrust and fear the other communities who are your blood and flesh; to distrust you must side with the British and prolong our slavery, but to cooperate and give your good-will, will bring social order based on eternal principles of Justice, equality and fraternity.

Jai Hind

Yours etc.,

Eddie H. Pereira

Kisumu

1st April, 1946

THE GOAN VOICE

(Edited by Mr. Dominic de Souza, published by the Goan Welfare Leaque and printed by W. Boyd & Co., Ltd., Nairobi)

The term 'Gomantaki' or 'Gomantakies' is derived from Gomantak. The term was loosely applied and used in the period prior to both Indian and Goan liberation. It is often used in a nationalistic context of uniting Konkani-speaking people of Goa - Benegal Pereira.

20   **OUR PAPER**   September, 1946.

Secret Service Message: The Russian bear is nursing its brood of satellites. Suspected to be a case of breeding trouble.

*

Messrs. Peth-wick Lawrence, Cripps and Alexander roosted for three months in India and hatched the Constituent Assembly Fowl. Jinnah says it is really foul and won't touch it; the Sikhs won't nurse it. Will the Congress be its sole ma-bap?

*

Dr. Lohia went to Goa to assert freedom of speech and civil liberty. What is freedom of speech? asks a cynic. It is the miraculous performance of howling when your mouth is gagged and gagging

others when you are free. And what is civil liberty?" he again asks; and caustically adds "is it liberty to be civil or liberty to be uncivil?"

*

The special correspondent a rival weekly of "Sarcasm and Satire" reports: Mr. Creech Jones is making a whirlwind tour of East Africa. What stew or biriani or unga is he preparing? Will it satisfy all palates and all plates?

*

A new interpretation of Jehovah preaching to the Black Adams of East Africa: unless you are prepared to work harder than you do today you cannot progress or get the things you want."

WHAT READERS HAVE TO SAY . . .

TO THE GOMANTAKI YOUTH

Comrades! Jai Hind — This is the first time in the history of our settlement in East Africa that we have "OUR PAPER" the mouthpiece of the Gomantakies and I sincerely trust it will devote its pages mainly for political consumption and as a reader I am unrestrainedly grateful for the championship of its liberties and privileges.

You know well that the destinies of the nations are moulded by the youth, they are the symbol of eternal energy that give birth to world famous revolutions that change the face of the earth, and like the ocean which has many precious gems at its bottom, the youth have their gems. Whenever and wherever a nation or a country is dissatisfied with its present status and feels

the degradation and injustice of bondage, away it looks with a hopeful eye to the flower of youth, the promise of the realization of its sweet and happy dreams. Comrades, we, youths, have our Mission, we have to arise and act. We know our failings, let us be up and doing. Wipe out those ugly and repulsive tendencies and customs that have knowingly or unknowingly crept amongst us. We have this noble cause of selfless service to our community and country. The hour is struck and we must have it on the anvil. Let us come about to work. We think we have been completely westernised and some of us even take pride in it; we look upon the West as our benefactors but comrades, don't forget that we are the sons of

EDITED BY MR. DOMINIC DE SOUZA, PUBLISHED BY THE GOAN WELFARE LEAGUE AND PRINTED BY W. BOYD & CO., LTD., NAIROBI.

Mother India, many of us were born and bred up there, we have only come here to earn our living and have a decent home but at the same time we have to keep in mind the obligations and indebitedness we owe to our Motherland. An Englishman wherever he is and in whatever circumstances he is, never forgets his mother England and that is the secret of his power, that is the unifying force that enables him to control us.

In taking stock of our patriotism we come to the painful realisation that we Gomantakies are politically starved and consequently reduced to a state of crumb-pickers, in contrast with the other communities who are in the ascendant, certainly so far as the good things of the world are concerned; they have money and education, they are wise enough to read the signs of the times, they are working for themselves while we Gomantakies are flirting with all sorts of Western life which is unnatural and grossly neglecting our own position. Being the sons of Bharat Mata we have to live and die as her sons and as things are to-day, when the British have so definitely "dethroned" themselves, there is no other party with which we will have to deal, than that of the Congress Party. What type of account are you going to render? please give thought to this serious question and you will feel the neglect for the fight for emancipation, therefore a big move will have to be made right now by developing strong rebellious spirit, otherwise we perish.

Comrades, there was a time when we as the Marathas were the only people in India with a prin-ciple of nationality, of course this is no longer true as we have lost ours and other genuine nations have emerged, what then has happened to us? Where has our vigorous nationalistic feeling disappeared? Into 435 years of subjection is the answer, Oh Lord, how long? the world in our own generation appears to be sinking, who can avert this catastrophe? are you prepared to sit down with folded arms while the youth of the other communities are marching towards emancipation with the splended and inspiring example of sacrifice and suffering before us of the Congress, I cannot believe it, we shall give loyal devotion to the cause of the common mother land and help in building up a united and indissoluble nation.

JAI HIND.
Kisumu,   Eddie H. Prereira.
20th July, 1946.

The Editor, "Our Paper".

Sir,—I feel highly elated in seeing the first issue of 'Our Paper' in its Christening Gown.

I have read it from cover to cover; there is in it the odour of the busy bee and many elegant touches of humour, both of which are signs of progress and mental development.

Its aim is inspiring and it will nevertheless encourage many of our budding writers to dig up their latent faculties.

I congratulate you on your new venture and sincerely wish your enterprise every success.

Yours etc.,
PATRICK FERREIRA.
Mombasa,
28.8.46.

To the Gomantaki Youth

Comrades! Jai Hind – This is the first time in the history of our settlement in East Africa that we have "OUR PAPER" the mouthpiece of the Gomantakies and I sincerely trust it will devote its pages mainly for political consumption and as a reader I am unrestrainedly grateful for the championship of liberties and privileges.

You know well that destines are moulded by the youth, they are the symbol of eternal energy that give birth to world famous revolution that change the face of the earth, and like the ocean which has many precious gems at its bottom, the youth have their gems. Whenever and wherever a nation or country is dissatisfied with its present status and feels the degradation and injustice of bondage, away it looks with a hopeful eye to the flower of youth, the promise of the realisation of its sweet and happy dreams. Comrades, we, youths, have our Mission, we have to arise and act. We know our failings, let us be up and doing. Wipe out those ugly and repulsive tendencies and customs that have knowingly or unknowingly crept amongst us. We have this noble cause of selfless service to our community and country. The hour is struck and we must have it on the anvil. Let us come about to work. We think we have been completely westernised and some of us even take pride in it; we look upon the West as our benefactors but comrades, don't forget that we are the sons of Mother India, many of us were born and bred up there, we have only come here to earn our living and have a decent home but at the same time we have to keep in mind the obligations and indebtedness we owe o our Motherland. An Englishman wherever he is and in whatever circumstances he is, never forgets his mother England and that is the secret of his power, that is the unifying force that enables him to control us.

In taking stock of our patriotism we come to the painful realisation that we Gomantakies are politically staved and consequently reduced to a state of crumb-pickers, in contrast with the other communities who are in the ascendant, certainly so far as so good things of the world are concerned; they have money and education, they are wise enough to read the signs of the times, they are working for themselves while Gomantakies are flirting with all sorts of Western life which is unnatural and grossly neglecting our own position. Being the sons of Bharat Mata, we have to live and die as her sons and as things are today, when the British have not definitely "dethroned" themselves, there is no other party with which we will have to deal, then that of the Congress Party. What type of account are you going to render? Please give thought to this serous question and you will feel the neglect for the fight for emancipation, therefore a big move will have to be made right now by developing strong rebellious spirit, otherwise we perish.

Comrades, there was a time when we as the Marathas were the only people in India with a principle of nationality, of course this is no longer true as we have lost ours and other genuine nations have emerged, what then has happened to us? Where has our vigorous nationalistic feeling disappeared? In 435 years of subjection is the answer, Oh Lord, how long? the world in our own generation appears to be sinking, who can avert this catastrophe? Are you prepared to sit down with folded arms while the youth of the other communities are marching towards emancipation with the splendour and inspiring example of sacrifice and suffering before us of the Congress, I cannot believe it, we shall give loyal devotion to the cause of the common motherland and help building up a united and indissoluble nation?

JAI HIND

Eddie H. Pereira

Kisumu,

20th July, 1946

FIFTH COLUMNISTS IN GOA

FIFTH COLUMNISTS IN GOA

Lisbon, December 1.

A political statue for Goa, which would give that possession the same status as a Province of Metropolitan Portugal, has been demanded by Dr. Floraino Melo, Indian intellectual and Deputy for Goa in the National Assembly. Frequent cheers interrupted the Indian Deputy as he spoke of conditions in Goa.

Goa "is surrounded by hostile atmosphere," Dr. Melo said, adding "it is necessary to make known to all the peoples and governments of the world that our India is and will continue to be Portuguese and to destroy forever the legend that Portuguese territory requires British India to enable to it live and subsist."

Referring to the unrest in Goa. Dr. Melo explained that this was caused by a few "Fifth Columnists and Nazis, and intellectuals educated in Central Europe and fanatics who had failed in life, who preach the absorption of Goa and foment hatred to the Portuguese Nation."

The National Assembly unanimously approved a motion of solidarity with the Government and people of Goa. (Reuter.)

The resistance against imperialism gathered momentum as the 1940s progressed. Two years after the Second World War ended, Indian independence (1947) marked a most significant watershed in history. The Indian freedom struggle had for long touched off similar struggles across the Indian Ocean, and it spilled over into Kenya. At the outset of the decade it had inspired nationalistic activists in both Africa and Indian subcontinent; now there was a new surge at hand. France, Portugal, even Britain, would try desperately to hang on to their old possessions; and in them both rulers and their toadies would make a formidable fist. Portugal's prime minister Salazar, claimed that Goa - its territory on the Indian subcontinent - was not a colony, and an essential part of Portugal. Salazar's assertion led Dr. Floriano de Mello, Member of the Portuguese National Assembly for Goa (on the western coast of India) to make a bold declaration that a political statute had been passed giving Goa the same status as metropolitan Lisbon. Goan nationalists, both at home and abroad (referred to as Gomantakies -- Konkani-speaking), strongly argued with response. Sad to say, in places such as Kenya, the nationalists were reviled; but they fought the resistance through the press, and finally triumphed. Letters to *The Colonial Times* newspaper (Nairobi) chronicle the indignity of the proponents of colonialism and records the brave opposition to them by the freedom fighters. - Benegal Pereira

Eddie Pereira responds to a Reuter news item from Lisbon, December 1. 1946

FIFTH COLUMNISTS IN GOA

Sir, -- Jai Hind. Who is this Dr. Floraino Melo, "Indian intellectual and Deputy for Goa in the Portuguese National Assembly?" Sir, he is a vulture feeding on the carcass of a rotting Portuguese Empire, a Windbag, dissembling traitor, and an open enemy, who is guilty of an unpardonable levity.

This Asiatic Quisling states that, "Goa is surrounded by hostile atmosphere," indeed it is and shall continue hostile towards the Portuguese Imperialists, Nazis and Barbarians. It is time that the Portuguese learn to view their record in Gomantak more objectively than has been their habit in the past. It ought to be recognised and understood that Portugal has ruined Gomantak's prosperity, manliness, culture, religion, arrested her economic development and kept poor, loving Gomantak in abject misery as one vast rural slum. She shall however, rise to glory again.

Referring to the unrest in Goa, Quisling Melo explained that, "it is due to the fifth Columnist". This statement is an irony for the Gods to laugh, provocating an insult to National Gomantak. Such tactics may deceive the foreign public but only amuse the Gomantakies. If it can crush the National Movement, I have a blue print for the invasion of Mars.

Our time shall come to Settle Accounts with Quislings and we shall not forget to demand an Account from this unworthy son who has sunk to the depths of distortion and fabrication, to be brought before a tribunal of an independent and national Gomantak.

Long live our glorious Motherland, its Revolution for a free and Independent Gomantak.

Jai Hind

Your etc

Eddie H. Pereira

Elburgon,

7th December, 1946

Portuguese Metropolitan Status for Goa

Sir – The caption strikes one in the eye as pompous and which is the outcome of storms in a teacup of the Portuguese bureaucracy as circumstantial evidence certainly suggest.

All the foreigners will agree that the Portuguese are a stupid race and to confirm their stupidity, here is their latest declaration; GOA HAS A STATUS OF METROPOLITAN PORTUGAL". This declaration is meaningless and un-understandable. Gomantak differs from Portugal as the North Pole does from the South Pole.

The Gomantakies know no other home or metropolis, save the few yards of space, which they possess in the land of sorrow and tears. Gomantak's freedom cannot exist within the orbit of imperialism, Portuguese metropolitan status or any other status within the foreign structure is wholly inapplicable to Gomantak.

The struggle of Gomantak is for liberty to roam freely in its land. Indulge in every kind of civil liberty, give expression to every kind of thought and action, and to promulgate social, economic and cultural activity. Does this exist today? Not even a ghost of it and instead of ushering this prosperity, new chains of slavery are replaced for the few snapped by the national movement!!
Jai Hind
Yours etc.
Eddie H. Pereira
Elburgon.
4th January 1947

"Pro Patria, Where Art Thou?

Sir, - Judas, I spit on your face. Pro Patria, why don't you call yourself Traitor? You have not the courage to reveal your name or identity and ordinarily an anonymous letter would receive but little attention.

Let me get down and entertain your audacity.

1. "Pro Patria" thinks I am a hater of European races – I am glad he has labeled me so. He would have done better justice had he referred to the dictionary for a stronger word than hater. In 1947 only a traitor can come out in praise of Imperialism.

2. "Pro Patria" informs us that Portugal is the oldest ally of Great

Britain and has fought by the side of the British in two world wars. You tell that to your British masters, National Gomantak is not interested. Our people have perished of hunger during these wars and not even a cart load of rice was delivered.

3. "Pro Patria" says that I am out to create mischief. If I attempt to speak the truth about the treatment to Gomantakies met by their Portuguese masters, I should not be blamed for teaching the down trodden.

4. "Pro Patria" says the Goans are unanimously happy at the news of the Political Statute granted. It is hardly necessary for me to ask your Gomantak readers to BEWARE OF BUYING THE P.M.S. EGGS. "Pro Patria" thinks that the whole of Gomantak is void of common sense as not to understand the hocus-pocus declaration of stupidity, delivered to us by the Traitor Floriano Melo and his chief agent in Kampala, Pro Patria. If the declaration has blessed Gomantak with civil liberties and chased away slavery, starvation and exploitation why are our national leaders, namely Braganza, Dr. Ramrao

Hegde, Kakodkar, Loyala and Bhembra rotting in Portuguese prisons. Does "Pro Patria" mean to tell us that these leaders are enjoying the delicious recipes of Portuguese Metropolitan Status?

Liberty, where art thou! I salute you.

Jai Hind.

Yours etc.
Eddie H. Pereira

Elburgon.
17th February 1947

Nazmi Durrani: Biographical Notes

Teresa Ongaro: Death of a Dear Friend[12]

None of us was prepared for the tragic and untimely death of Nazmi Durrani, with whom we had cycled all day through Nairobi's suburbs on Sunday 1st July, [1990] the climax of the Uvumbuzi Bicycle Awareness Campaign. We were dispersing in different directions after a hearty lunch when it happened. Nazmi left Uhuru Park for home peddling towards town with a group of friends. Shortly afterwards we received news that he had been hit by a bus on Kenyatta Avenue near Serena Hotel. He was immediately rushed to Nairobi Hospital where he was pronounced dead on arrival. We received news of Nazmi's death with shock, horror and disbelief. Why, why, why…

Nazmi became a member of Uvumbuzi just over a year ago. His first involvement with the Club was participation in the 1988 Bikathon. He attended all meetings, excursions, bashes, tree planting exercises and camping trips--notably the Okavango Trip in October 1989. His friendly outgoing

---

12. Ongaro, Teresa: The Swinging Seventeen. *Uvumbuzi Tales & Trails*. Special Edition. (1989)

manner earned him respect and affection all round. At 48 years of age, he was the oldest member of the Club, and one of the most active. For his untiring involvement in Uvumbuzi activities he was awarded Chairman's prize for Most Active Member in 1989. At the 1990 Annual General Meeting Nazmi was elected Committee member, a position he held until the time of his death.

Through Uvumbuzi Nazmi developed a keen interest in cycling, especially as a means of keeping fit. He had two bicycles of which he was always willing to lend one. He sat on the 1990 Bicycle Committee which is charged with responsibility for both the Bicycle Awareness Day and the Annual Magadi Bikathon. He cycled faithfully every Sunday distributing pre-Bicycle Day literature to wananchi all over town, and was instrumental in preparation of the Kiswahili translations.

I remember Nazmi with deep fondness. He was like an older brother to all of us. He had a way with people, could unbend you so easily and was always so sensitive to other people's feelings. Everyone was important as the next person to Nazmi, yet somehow he made you feel very special. His love for children was boundless. He was always dependable, and went about his business with great dedication. And his anecdotes were a constant source of amusement for many of us. He was a pillar of strength and wisdom in Uvumbuzi, giving guidance and encouragement in all affairs--work, personal, Club... Nazmi wanted to see Uvumbuzi involved in conservation of wildlife and environment, and also of local languages, values and traditions--culture. Nazmi had very strong feelings against apartheid, maintaining a keen interest in the developments in South Africa.

Even as we highlight the environmental, health and economical benefits of cycling, the issue of road safety for cyclists is never far from our mind. Part of the emphasis of the Bicycle Awareness Campaign is on the need for separate cyclist paths to keep motor vehicles away. Until such time as this is achieved, cyclists will continue to be at great risk.

He was plucked from our midst, and like the light of a candle Nazmi's life was snuffed out. Already we miss you terribly Nazmi, and we shall always cherish our memories of you.

Nekesa
July 1990

Shiraz Durrani: Nazmi Durrani, Highlights of an Activist's Life[13]

Nazmi was born in Kisumu, Kenya on March 31, 1942 and died in an accident in Nairobi on July 1, 1990. He was the third child of Gulamhussein and Shirin Durrani both of whom were born in Nairobi. Nazmi's grandfather, Alibhai Ramji, (on his father's side) was born in Jam Timby, Naunagar State, India in 1890 and later married Avalbai. He came to Kenya when he was about 10 years old. Alibhai's father, Ramji Kanji, had sent Alibhai (and later his younger brother) to Kenya following drought and impoverishment due to British oppression of Indian peasants.

Nazmi studied at the Aga Khan Secondary School and Allidina Visram High School in Mombasa prior to graduating in 1965 at the University of Leicester in England. Following a Post Graduate Diploma in Education at Makerere University in Kampala, Uganda in 1966, Nazmi taught at the Aga Khan High School in Mombasa before moving to Nairobi where he worked at the Library of Congress Office from 1969 until his death on July 1, 1990

In that brief working period of 24 years, Nazmi developed many interests. The selection of his writing in this book provides a glimpse into the range of his interests and work. However, it misses out the main motive that powered his writing and the vast range of his activities. While Nazmi was a left-leaning progressive intellectual, he did not come to his own until he became a member of the underground political organisation, The December Twelve Movement, towards the end of 1970s. Joining the anti-imperialist organisation helped him to make the transition from a left-leaning intellectual to a political activist

---

13. Source: Shiraz Durrani. *Opinion*. 09-06-2016. Available at: http://opinionmagazine. co.uk/details/2053/nazmi-durrani-highlights-of-an-activist's-life. [Accessed: 11-10-16].

who directed his energy to working for a just and more equal Kenya. This is the struggle that motivated him until his untimely and tragic death.

As a librarian, Nazmi was aware of the central role that relevant information could play in the struggle to liberate the minds of working people from a mindset moulded by imperialism. As a teacher, he was keen to ensure that the learning and experience he had were passed on to others, particularly the younger generation growing up under neo-colonialism. As a member of the December Twelve Movement, he was active in strengthening the organisational structures which could provide a powerful force to dislodge the imperialist-imposed culture and politics in Kenya. One of the causes in which Nazmi became active was the environmental movement which embraced causes that served the needs of working people, such as campaigns to develop bicycle lanes in Nairobi so that workers could have a safe and viable means of transport to and from work.

In addition, Nazmi also became involved in cultural activities as an arm of the liberation struggle in which he was active. Along with other activists, he was against the imposition of English as the only viable language in Kenya. He thus learned Kiswahili and wrote stories, poems and historical pieces in Kiswahili so as to reach workers who used this medium of communication. Some of his poems in Kiswahili are reproduced in this book, but a more substantial collection of his resistance poetry in Kiswahili will be published under the title *Tunakataa* in 2017. At the same time, he supported the use of the languages of Kenyan nationalities. In this context, he sharpened his skills in his own mother tongue, Gujarati, and wrote historical and cultural articles that would increase awareness among Gujarati-speaking people. Some of his articles written and published in Gujarati are reproduced in this book. He also wrote a play in Gujarati, *Katokati no Samai* and translated it into English under the title *An Encounter in Eastleigh*. To date, the English version remains to be published. He also devised also some crosswords in Gujarati for *Alakmalak* magazine. He wrote stories, puzzles and other learning material for children, some published in *Alakmalak*, while others were given to younger members of his own family.

Many of his activities, particularly political ones, remain to be documented. One such activity was the the use of his house in the Ngara area of Nairobi as a safe house for political work of the December Twelve Movement and the setting up of the liberation library there. The "secret basement in a house", mentioned below was Nazmi's, as recorded by Durrani, S.[14]:

> Another way in which the Library Cell met the needs of the people was writing, printing and distributing underground pamphlets. Thus a number of underground pamphlets were cyclostyled by Cell members using a secret basement in a house in the [Ngara] area of Nairobi. The house itself had been a "safe" underground facility for a number of political activities, including a venue for safe meetings. It also housed the Movement's library which served as a central reference centre for the movement. The "Notes accompanying donation of books to Cuba" (Durrani, 2008) in 2000, provide further details on the library:
>
>> Thus the liberation forces of necessity had to set up their own underground liberation libraries. Perhaps the largest one was the one run by Nazmi Durrani which provided a major reference point for December Twelve Movement which published its own newspaper Pambana ("Struggle") in early 1980s. The library contained material which was banned in Kenya and which could lead to indefinite detention if found out. This included works of Marx, Lenin, Stalin, Castro, as well as publications from USSR and the Foreign Language Press in Beijing.

14. Durrani, Shiraz (2014): Progressive Librarianship: Perspectives from Kenya and Britain, 1979-2010. London: Vita Books.

This library also provided the source material for important documents in the fight against the neo-colonial Moi regime such as Mwakenya's Register of Resistance (1987), and Umoja(1989)[15].

In Progressive Librarianship, Durrani, S. provides some background to Nazmi's articles in this book:

Library Cell members were active in other areas as well. One method they used was the use of open publishing avenues to create a new awareness of the history of resistance. An important contribution was that of Nazmi Durrani writing as Nazmi Ramji for security reasons. He worked as a librarian at the Library of Congress in Nairobi, but developed December Twelve Movement's (DTM) library in a secret location. As a member of the Library Cell, he participated in all its information activities, as well as in all DTM political work. He also acted as Kanoru in Ngugi wa Thiongo's play Maitu Njugira (Translated as "Mother Sing for me", 1981) which was banned by the Kenya Government who then detained the author… He [Nazmi] was also responsible for compiling a number of publications circulating underground. These included Article 5 – Human Rights Violations [in Kenya][16] and Upande Mwingine - collections of resistance activities by workers, peasants, students and others.

He also wrote and published a series of articles in Gujarati under the heading "Biographies of patriotic Asian Kenyans" which sought to counter the Government propaganda which painted South Asian communities in a very negative light. The series was written in Gujarati and published in the Gujarati magazine, Alakmalak.

15. Umoja (1989): Moi's Reign of Terror: a Decade of Nyayo Crimes Against the People of Kenya. London: Umoja (Umoja wa kupigania Demokrasia Kenya/United Movement for Democracy in Kenya).
16. Refers to Article 5 of Universal Declaration on Human Rights.

At a personal level, Nazmi remained down-to-earth and perfectly at home with all - children, youth, older people. Teresa Ongaro[17] captures Nazmi's personality:

> If Nazmi Durrani thought his grey hair would earn him some reverence on this trip, he must have been very disappointed—to us he was just one of the guys! His sense of humour, his modesty and his generosity (one cold night in Francistown, Nazmi let someone sleep in his sleeping bag who hadn't even asked!) made him a favourite among us all. To Nazmi, solitude is for sleeping—two minutes on his own and he'd be dreaming away to glory. This trancelike state soon came to be known as Nazmititis. His endless wit provided us a regular source of comedy. However, Nazmi's leadership qualities are doubtful—his suggestion of a venue for a meal led to the near decimation of our group's male species.

In one of his poems[18], Nazmi asks:

When shall we liberate
Ourselves from this mental slavery?

The struggle to liberate people's minds from the imperialist mental slavery became Nazmi's lifelong pursuit.

---

17. Ongaro, Teresa: The Swinging Seventeen. *Uvumbuzi Tales & Trails*. Special Edition. (1989)
18. Why and When - To be included in the forthcoming book of resistance poems by Nazmi, *Tunakataa!* Reproduced in this book.

Nazmi, the Actor

Nazmi acting in the play "Maitu Njugira" (Mother Sing For Me) by Ngugi wa Thiong'o staged in 1982. Directed by Waigwa Wachiira and Kimani Gecau. Wednesday August 8, 1990

Sunday July 1 this year was Uvumbuzi Bicycle Awareness Day. In outstanding weather, 50 cyclists rode through various Nairobi neighbourhoods to promote the benefits of cycling. Police escorts, with hazard lights ablaze, cleared a safe path. Young and old cycled side by side. Men and women from all walks of life spread the message widely: "Save Money, Save the Environment; Cycle Now!". With traffic halted between the Railway Station and Uhuru Highway, we rolled into Uhuru Park to complete the tour with a picnic celebration. The event was a resounding success.

Wednesday, August 8, 1990.   Nazmi

Some members of Uvumbuzi club, ready for action in one of their many events recently.

But a sad and poignant point was proven that afternoon. Our roads currently are not safe - especially for cyclists. One of the leading organizers of the day's events was tragically killed while pedalling home from Uhuru Park. The police escorts had gone home; we were now ordinary cyclists under our own guard.

Nazmi Durrani became one of the most enthusiastic advocates of bicycles in Uvumbuzi Club (an indigenous environmental and wildlife education group) translating pamphlets into Kiswahili and riding to various Nairobi estates each Sunday for weeks before Bicycle Awareness Day in a promotional entourage. He insisted on riding his bike to the event that fateful day when offered a ride by car.

Nekesa and Rahim Suleman:
Uvumbuzi Tales & Trails

UVUMBUZI TALES & TRAILS
No. 6 July 1990

Uvumbuzi members learned of the untimely passing of Nazmi Durrani with deep shock and sorrow. On 1st July 1990 Uvumbuzi Club organised some fifty cyclists to ride around Nairobi streets distributing leaflets promoting the environmental and economic benefits of cycling as well as appealing to motorists to give due recognition and respect to cyclists. We were asking wananchi to abandon cars, buses and matatus in favour of bicycles - and we meant it. Our next step was to campaign for a bicycle infrastructure in the city...

But the enthusiasm was short-lived. Not long after we dispersed. Nazmi, one of the leading supporters of the Bicycle Awareness Campaign was fatally injured after being hit by a bus while pedalling home with a group of friends.

The tragedy of Nazmi's death calls for an urgent shift in the focus of the Bicycle Awareness Campaign. We must demonstrate to the relevant ministries and authorities that while the bicycle can give crucial mobility to thousands of commuters while demanding little from the economy and the environment, the safety of the cyclist is paramount. Separate cyclist paths are a must to keep motor vehicles away, and those perilous potholes must go. Uvumbuzi Club must do something to see that positive steps are taken to insure the safely of cyclists on our roads. Only then can we dare promote the use of bicycles by wananchi. We owe it to Nazmi...

Naznudeen Durrani was born in Kisumu on 31 March 1942. After completing his primar education at City Primary School, Nairobi he went to Aga Khan High school, Mombasa where he did both is O" and A' levels. He did a BA at Leicester University, England and later Makerere University, Uganda. He taught for a year at his former high school, then joined the US Embassy Library of Congress where he worked as a librarian from 1969 to the time of his death. Nazmi became a member of the Uvumbuzi Club just over a year ago. His first involvement with the club was participation in 1988 Bikathon. Through Uvumbuzi he developed a keen interest in cycling, especially for fitness and leisure, and was soon highly involved in the Bicycle Awareness Campaign. He always encouraged non-cyclists to learn; and urged everyone to acquire and ride bicycles. What tragic irony that Nazmi should meet his death on a bicycle on Bicycle awareness Day - he had not brought his car that day simply because he could ride home.

Some of Nazmi's greatest satisfaction came from his experiences with Uvumbuzi. We will remember his enthusiasm for outings with Mama Fatuma's children; visits to Thogoto Home for the Aged. Maanzoni Primary School; tree planting sessions; and exclusions: Lake Baringo, Menengai, Okavango, Ruiru Dam, Shaba... to name a few. He will be remembered likewise for his deep commitment to the liberation of South Africa, and earlier on. Namibia. Independence Day in Namibia was a great day in Nazmi's life. A frequent visitor at the theatre. Nazmi had a keen interest in poetry, drama and traditional music, both in his mother tongue Gujarati and in Kiswahili. He promoted his mother tongue among his friends and was forever going on at us to speak, read and write in Kiswahili. He wrote a poem for each issue of the Uvumbuzi newsletter.

Nazmi, who was a bachelor, is survived by a sister and brother, nephews and nieces and many friends with whom he had a close relationship. He had a most generous heart, a wonderful sense of humour and he was, above all, a good person. concerned and sensitive to the needs of others.

For those of us fortunate enough to know him, Nazmi was a friend, companion and gentleman through and through a shining example of what we should aspire In be.

Nekesa & Rahim

Why & When - A Poem by Nazmi[19]

The foreign invaders came
And conquered our countries
Their gun was more powerful
Than our spear and arrow.
On the superiority of this
One murderous weapon
Was built a monumental myth
Of continental and racial superiority.
And this was drummed into
Our heads in their schools
And there it still remains.

Their population is made up of peoples
Ours of tribes.
Their colour signifies purity
Ours darkness and death.
They live in houses
We in huts.
Theirs are languages
Ours vernaculars.
Their superstitions are religion
Our beliefs paganism.
Their medicinemen are doctors
Our witch-doctors.
They are ruled by laws
We by mere customs.
Their culture is civilization
Ours is made up of traditions.

---

19. Included in the forthcoming book of resistance poems by Nazmi Durrani, *Tunakataa*.

What they think and say
Is their problem, not ours.
But the 'Why' I have is:
Why should we describe
Ourselves in their terms?
When shall we liberate
Ourselves from this mental slavery?
—

In Memory of Nazmi...

In memory of Nazmi...

A tree planting ceremony will take place at Thogoto Tree Nursery on Saturday 25 August 1990 at 11.00am.

The Bicycle Awareness Day will be held every first Sunday of July, and will be dedicated to the memory of Nazmi.

The Nazmi Durrani Trophy for the Most Active Member is being donated by a certain member to be awarded each year to a deserving member.

First Aid lessons are being arranged by Maryanne Kamau. Please contact her to register now.

IN LOVING MEMORY
NAZMI DURRANI

Other Books by Nazmi Durrani

Katokati no Samai

Encounter in Eastleigh-
English version of *Katokati no Samai*

Forthcoming
Tunakataa: Resistance Poems

In Kiswahili with English
Translations by the Author
By
Nazmi Durrani

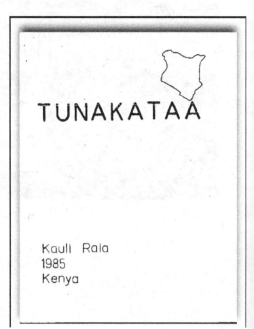

Index of Selected Terms / પસંદ શબ્દો અનુક્રમણિકા

Indexing the Bigger Picture

The Index in this book is not meant to be a comprehensive record of all names, places, events and incidents mentioned in the book. It has been created for another purpose - as a pointer to the wider context of the world and impact that the progressive South Asian Kenyans have had. A quick glance at the Index indicates that they were by no means an isolated group of people operating in a vacuum. One of the authors, Naila Durrani, mentions the fact that the South Asian communities made up a very tiny proportion of the total population of Kenya. And the progressive people within this already small group was indeed few. Yet their impact was profound on the struggle and history of Kenya. The Index may help to explain the reasons for this small number of people having such a big impact.

The Index focuses attention on the complex world of the individuals and groups mentioned in this book. It highlights a number of areas from which this group got its inspiration, in which it operated and which it influenced. A few of these are mentioned here.

The issues that inspired this group included land, employment, freedom, banks, industry and firms and indicated the anti-imperialist demands of the people. The range of countries named in the Index reveals the internationalism of the group: India, Canada, UK, Ethiopia, Goa, Mozambique, Uganda.

The organisations mentioned indicate their understanding of the need for having a united organisation under a common ideology as well as their links with international organisations: Mozambique African National Movement, Labour Trade Union of East Africa, Kikuyu Central Association, Kenya Freedom Party, Kenya African Study Union, Indian Workers Union, Ghadar Party, Freedom Committee of OAU, All Africa Trade Union Federation, Mau Mau. Their links with the various African organisations, including the ones mentioned under Organisation, and individuals indicate that they were in fact part of the wider national movement for the liberation of Kenya, by no means an isolated group focussed solely on issues that affected their own communities. Their class and professional affiliations indicate that they represented a broad spectrum of people: trade unionists, lawyers, doctors, artisans, etc. Their methods to achieve their aims included the use of newspapers, posters, leaflets, books, culture, language and involvement in various aspects of the Mau Mau armed struggle.

The picture that emerges from the above is that this group of activists may have been small in number but their world was large and all-encompassing. They fought for all Kenyans but particularly for the working people. All this indicated a need for a wider study to be done in order to set the progressive South Asian Kenyan activists in an inclusive perspective. This would embrace national as well as class struggles in Kenya so that Kenya's history reflects the fuller picture and nature of the anti-colonialist and anti-imperialist struggle.

Shiraz Durrani

Index

Vita Books Publications List

	Ngugi wa Thiong'o: Writing against Neocolonialism. 1986. 978-1-869886-00-4 *Out of Print.*
	Durrani, Shiraz: Kimaathi, Mau Mau's First Prime Minister of Kenya.1986. 978-1-869886-01-1
	Karimi Nduthu: A Life in the Struggle. 1998. Vita Books & Mau Mau Research Centre. ISBN: 978-1-869886-12-7. Available from MMRC.
	Durrani, Shiraz: Never Be Silent: Publishing and Imperialism in Kenya, 1886-1963. 2006. ISBN: 978-1-869886-05-9
	Durrani, Shiraz. Progressive Librarianship: Perspectives from Britain and Kenya. 2014. 978-1-869886-12-7 (print); ISBN: 978-1-869886-13-4 (digital)
	Durrani, Shiraz (Comp.): Makhan Singh, A Revolutionary Kenyan Trade Unionist. 2015. ISBN: 978-1-869886-22-6
	Durrani, Nazmi; Durrani, Naila; Pereira, Benegal: Liberating Minds, Restoring Kenyan History: Anti-Imperialist Resistance by Progressive South Asian Kenyans, 1884-1965. 2016. ISBN: 978-9966-097-41-5
	Vita Posters: Kimaathi / Muthoni / Arms & Struggle. *Out of print.*

New Book Announcement · 2017

Pio Gama Pinto, the Assassinated Hero of the Anti-Imperialist Struggle in Kenya. 1927 - 1965

Compiled by

Shiraz Durrani

ISBN:
978-9966-1890-0-4

Published to mark Pio Gama Pinto's assassination on February 24, 1965, the book consists of an assessment of his political life by Shiraz Durrani who looks at the social and political context of Pinto's life and death. The two-line struggle in Kenya forms the backdrop to Pinto's life. Durrani examines Pinto's work in various organisations, in the struggles for land, trade unions and Mau Mau.

As material on Pinto has been lost, "disappeared" or destroyed, the book reproduces some of Pinto's surviving articles and reproduces the now out of print tribute to him, *Pio Gama Pinto, Independent Kenya's First Martyr*. It also includes views on him by Fenner Brockway, Malcolm MacDonald, Joseph Murumbi and Makhan Singh.

Pinto in his own words:

"It had become increasingly obvious that 'constitutional', 'non-violent' methods of fighting for one's rights were absolutely futile in dealing with the Settler-Colonial administration. ORGANISED VIOLENCE WAS THE ONLY ANSWER TO SUCH A SITUATION".

"The sacrifices of the hundreds of thousands

of Kenya's freedom fighters must be honoured by the effective implementation of the policy - a democratic, African, socialist state in which the people have the right to be free from economic exploitation and the right to social equality. Kenya's uhuru must not be transformed into freedom to exploit, or freedom to be hungry and live in ignorance. Uhuru must be uhuru for the masses - uhuru from exploitation, from ignorance, disease and poverty."

"Pinto was assassinated by the regime on 24 February 1965 and Kenya has yet to replace him" - Donald Barnett (1972).

John K. Tettegah (All Afr. TU Fed.):
"Pio Pinto fell on the battlefield in our common war against neo-colonialism... Along with the immortal Patrice Lumumba, ... he has joined the ranks of martyrs whose blood must be avenged. ... his death will recruit new armies of Pintos to continue the fight in which he died, the effort to create a united socialist Africa".

CONTENTS

Foreword: **Willy Mutunga and Pheroze Nowrojee.**
Pio Gama Pinto:
Autobiographical Sketch; A Detainee's Life Story.

Emma Gama Pinto: Remembering Pio.

Shiraz Durrani: Pio Gama Pinto.

Pio Gama Pinto, Independent Kenya's First Martyr, Socialist & Freedom Fighter. (1966).

P. O. Box 62501-00200 Nairobi, Kenya
info.vitabkske@gmail.com
http://vitabooks.co.uk

Distributed Worldwide by:
African Books Collective
P.O.Box 721 Oxford, OX1 9EN UK
http://www.africanbookscollective.com

Notes & Quotes Series
Available at: http://vitabooks.co.uk/vita-books/publication-list/

Politics of Information: the Role of Alternative Information in Liberation Struggle. Discussion led by Shiraz Durrani. RPP. Nairobi. September 10, 2016. **Notes & Quotes Study Guide No. 3.** ISBN 978-1-869886-016-5

Mau Mau the Revolutionary Force From Kenya. by Shiraz Durrani. **Notes & Quotes Study Guide. 2. 2014.** ISBN 978-1-869886-03-5

Every inch a fighter: reflections on Makhan Singh and the trade union struggle in Kenya. by Shiraz Durrani. **Notes & Quotes Study Guide No. 1.** 2013. ISBN 978-1-869886-02-8

Vita Books

P.O.Box 62501-00200 Nairobi. Kenya
http://vitabooks.co.uk
email: info.vitabkske@gmail.com
info@vitabooks.co.uk

Distributed Worldwide by: African Books Collective
PO BOX 721
Oxford, OX1 9EN
orders@africanbookscollective.com
www.africanbookscollective.com

Printed in the United States
By Bookmasters